The Golden Years In Ministry

The Golden Years In Ministry

Finishing Well
As
Pastor, Minister, or Missionary
By
Allan Rodney Tilley

Dedication

This book is dedicated to all those pastors, ministers, missionaries, and servants of Jesus who are endeavoring to end well. I want to thank many of you who have shown me how to start and finish with a thankful heart and an open hand. You have been a great example to all of me personally. For those of you who are not doing well, I dedicate myself to praying for you, and to try and encourage you to be all that Christ Jesus desires you to be. May we cross the finish line together with a *well done, good, and faithful servant.*

Table of Contents

Introduction

"How many times have I told my wife that I have got to put it all down, but what will the church do?"

These new young pastors just don't get it"

"I am so confused. Some people keep telling me to stay while others keep telling me to leave or else they are leaving, and they are. They are voting with their feet"

"I have been here for fifty years, now what am I supposed to do, just curl up and die?"

"My health is failing, and I know it, but I am going to work till Jesus comes."

"The church is falling apart, and I am afraid of what is going to happen."

"Now that my wife died, I feel so alone. Now what?"

"This is my church. I started it and I am going to finish the course."

"I opted out of social security and do not have a dollar to my name. I gave the church everything, but no one cares if I live or die. Now that is gratitude for you!"

"The other day, right in the middle of the sermon, I forgot where I was going. It was so embarrassing. Everybody was nice about it, but it is

time to give it all up and stay at home and watch the preachers on the television. I do not know if I can go back."

"Can I admit it? Honestly, I just don't want to die. I know what life is and I think I know what death is going to be, but it is all so unsure. I have talked about it all my days as a pastor, but it feels more imminent than I thought it would be now that I am older. I am afraid."

There comes a time in everyone's life when you know it is almost over. It is a scary time of the unknown and unwanted. It is a time of confusion and loss, and now you have come face to face with the aging process that has ceased to motivate you, and confusion sets in. You feel hollow, sometimes alone, and the purpose that once drew you in, now only causes you to doubt your ability to survive. It can be a time of doubt, a time of asking the hard questions but receiving only fickle, trite answers, answers that get lost in your ability to think it all through.

Sometimes you just sit and look off into the distant horizons with the understanding that you are not getting more healthy or intellectually sharp, however, you still hold onto the desire that you can make a difference, and you want to finish well. You feel that as a pastor, many times you burned the candle at both ends as you did the work of the ministry, but now it appears that the candle is only smoldering, sending up spirals of smoke in a final desperate act of moving forward. As a minister, you have been upfront, leading, praying, encouraging, and now the only encouragement you receive is the wag of your dog's tail as you pat him on his head. You have given all to God and the church and you do not seek to be recognized, but just acknowledged and not ignored, and you feel so forgotten. You fight between leaving a legacy and just leaving. You like what you do, but not as much as in the past, or so it seems. Where is the passion? Where is the calling now? Do I still have what it takes and if not, what do I do? What is a pastor to do in a situation where you are too young to die but too old to continue?

I know it may sound pessimistic, but I have witnessed many pastors who have given up and taken the path of least resistance and laid it all down, never to take it up again. However, it is not over, it is different. It is not over; it is just moving into the unknown. Unknown to us, but not unknown to God. It is still a time of continued growth both spiritually and emotionally. You were once the "go-to" for the community and the church as they sought your advice and counsel with daily life struggles, but now they have found a new friend, and that really hurts.

According to Dr. Scott Nelson and Dr. E. Fuller Torrey, today's culture is turning to the psychiatrist, therapy groups, counselors, and sensitivity groups to lead them to a higher level of spiritual awareness.

Recently at an APA conference, they said, *"many of the qualities once attributed to rabbis, ministers, and priests by persons seeking a 'mediator of the unknown' are now attributed to the psychiatrist."* [1] As aging ministers, we are unsure of our role in the culture in which we find ourselves floundering, and therefore we too are seeking advice from others. But to whom does the pastor go? Who is the counselor's counselor? Who wants to put time into an aging pastor who is ready to be "put out to pasture."

In this book, we will look at ourselves, our fears, our hopes, and our very souls, to see how we can finish well, both at home here and there at our eternal home in heaven. We will explore our physical needs and our lack of adequate care, and we will also contemplate our future aspirations. We will ask our souls if the challenges forward can be met with hope and a godly expectation, or if life will lead only to despair. We will look at social concerns with both family and friends, and explore the nature of true community.

This is not an easy book to write and there are a vast array of books on aging, but few books have been written for aging pastors and those in the ministry. Many books have been written for the elderly concerning money management and the financial

---

[1] 125th American Psychiatric Association Conference, Dallas, Texas. USA.

desire to live out life in a secure manner. Other books on aging refuse to ask the hard questions and make up "senior moment" jokes trying to carry us through by laughing through the hard times. Then others go to the opposite extreme and only address the grief and loss and the preparation of the dead for burial. None of that sounds exciting or adequate and we do not need to dwell on the morbid as such, so in this book, I hope to address all of these issues from a pastoral perspective and see if, with a little thought and a little help, we can go from life to death with a *"well done good and faithful servant."* I, like most of you, want to finish well, but I am not sure we know what well is. Have I done it well, or have I been done over? Have I done anything of value that lasts or is it just a "passing in the night?"

Jesus many times said, *"He who had ears to hear, let him hear."* (Mark 4:9). And since it is a well-known fact that as you get older your ears physically continue to grow and get larger, Jesus, help us to listen largely to you, to others, and ourselves, so that we can hear and still obey. We still have ears, big ears, and Jesus, since you are still talking to us, help us to listen. Some of us will be listening with the assistance of hearing aids, and others are almost deaf, but Lord, we honestly ask you to speak again, touch again, and fill us again with your Holy Spirit and your presence. We need to know how to age and end well.

Chapter One
Well Done, but Not Over Cooked

The "Diagnostic and Statistical Manual of Mental Disorders" (DSM-5) of the American Psychiatric Association, endeavors to boil down pastoral retirement and ministry to a "Phase of Life Problem" (V62.89 – Z60.0), and reduce it to a life-cycle transition such as marriage or completing school, or getting a job, but we know it is so much more.

Retirement out of pastoral ministry is not a "forty years and a gold watch" moment, for our entire lifestyle, personal significance, and divine calling is taken into question. Yes, it is like a new career change, and yes, it is like adjusting to the "empty nest" syndrome, and yes, it is like taking a sabbatical, and yes, it is like taking a medical and health leave, but it is not just that. It is so much more. Ministry is similar to the story of Moses and the burning bush experience, where Moses verbally hears God's call to take his place in leadership and lead the entire nation of Israel out of Egypt. We, like Moses, felt it was a divine position, a God job, a "calling" that only pastors feel, and they do. But many times, out of that, again like Moses, comes arrogance, not authority, that says we are different from all the rest of humankind. We are better, higher, and more important than the everyday person on the street. We do not need to be challenged or confronted with our decisions. We know. We are God's messengers, and we have the message as well. That may not be vocalized, but when we lose that sense of purpose, we feel that the world, especially the church world, cannot do without us. However, Moses at the end of his ministry became the humblest man who ever lived as stated in Numbers 12:3, and we must do the same if we are going to end well.

Therefore, when we lose special status, we cannot fight back, and we cannot become angry, or even bitter as we see our lives lose their elevated status. We ask, "How can we now be just a congregant? How can we teach the "seniors class" and that be enough?" We struggle and become confused and strike out at God and man. However, there must be some changes we must implement in our thinking both spiritually and emotionally. All through the Bible others have struggled with the same feelings, and they too had to make drastic changes.

The Bible talks of old age and how we should be honored, *"You shall rise before the gray-headed and honor the presence of an old man, and fear your God: I am the Lord."* (Leviticus 19:32)

It also speaks of the glory of old age, *"The silver-headed head is a crown of glory, If it is found in the way of righteousness."* (Proverbs 16:31).

Psalm 92:12-15 says, *"The righteous shall flourish like a palm tree, He shall grow like a cedar of Lebanon. Those who are planted in the house of the Lord shall flourish in the courts of our God. They shall still bear fruit in old age; They shall be fresh and flourishing, To declare that the Lord is upright; He is my rock, and there is no unrighteousness in Him."*

Example after example exists throughout the Bible of men who, although old and apparently near death's door, can still be a lasting influence for God and his work, if only they change their thinking.

For example, Moses was to lead his people from Egypt into the promised land, but after forty years of traveling, Moses at the age of one hundred and twenty had the privilege to only view where he thought he was supposed to go. Just before Israel was to cross over the Jordan River, God led Moses up onto a mountain overlooking the land of promise and showed Moses where the others would go, but not Moses. Moses was going to die, and God was going to bury him, just shy of the purpose he had sought for years. I wonder what Moses felt. Did he cry and throw a fit of anger? Did he lash out at God and the other leaders? Did he appoint his eldest son to take his name and position? No, Moses, who was the humblest man who ever lived (Numbers 12:3), decided to take a better, higher road and he blesses the people, lays his hands on Joshua as his successor, and then leaves the world in dignity and peace. He showed us how it is to be done, even when *"His eyes were not dim, nor his natural vigor diminished."* (Deuteronomy 34:7b)

Another contemporary of Moses would be Caleb, who although he was eighty-five years of age, admonished Joshua, the commander for Moses, to allow him to go to the land of the Anakin, the giants of the time, and drive them out. As you can read from the passage in Joshua 14, Caleb sounds like an old war hero who is ready to take his WWII rifle, along with his helmet that was left in the garage, and go and defeat the enemy. It is a story Hollywood movies are made of. Joshua 14:7-12 reads, *"I was forty years old when Moses the servant of the Lord sent me from Kadesh Barnea to spy out the land, and I brought back word to him as it was in my heart. Nevertheless, my brethren who went up with me made the heart of the people melt, but I wholly followed the Lord my God. So, Moses swore on that day, saying, 'Surely the land where your foot has trodden shall be your inheritance and your children's forever, because you have wholly followed the Lord your God.' And now, behold, the Lord has kept me alive, as He said, these forty-five years, ever since the Lord spoke this word to Moses while Israel wandered in the wilderness; and now, here I am this day, eighty-five years old. As yet I am as strong this day as on the day that Moses sent me; just as my strength was then, so now is my strength for war, both for going and for coming in."* (Joshua 14:7-11).

I doubt Caleb's validation of his aging ministry was actually true for I have seen many elderly men who sound just like that, and who, at the same age as Caleb, have repeated stories of past vigor over and over again. We, as aging ministers, all do the same. But it does show us once again how we, as older men of ministry, feel when called upon to do something, anything, that would be helpful. We think we can do it, but everybody else knows we cannot, at least not in the same strength as when we were forty years of age. We talk like Caleb, but we live like a young buck with too many hormones, or at least try to.

And then, there is Joshua. What did Joshua do? He followed in Moses' footsteps and when he is a hundred and ten years old, he calls the people to himself and reminds them of what God has done, not what he had done.[2] Joshua did not dedicate a chapel in his name or set up a memorial to himself, but he challenged the people to serve God Jehovah, and him alone. He then sets up a covenant stone under a large tree to commemorate the words of the Lord that God spoke. It was not a monument to Joshua. He did not go into the promised land and rename the town of Jericho, Joshuaville, after his legacy. He emphasized the Word of God, not his own words. He did not continue to produce sermons and podcasts to keep his legacy going, but he only set up a stone to remember God's promises. He finished well.

These ancient patriarchs were secure in their aging

---

[2] Jeremiah, D. (2013). *The Jeremiah Study Bible*, New King James Version. Nashville, Tennessee: Thomas Nelson, Inc., p. 307.

and in their death and freely passed on all that they knew and blessed those that were to continue in God's legacy.

There were others as mentioned in the New Testament. The apostle Paul proclaims, *"I have fought the good fight, I finished the race, I have kept the faith. Finally, there is laid up for me the crown of righteousness, which the Lord, the righteous Judge, will give to me on that Day, and not to me only but also to all those who have loved His appearing."* (2 Timothy 4:16). He finished well. He authored the book of Philippians from his jail cell in Rome and relayed words of encouragement and joy to the church in Philippi.

"...being confident of this very thing, that He who has begun a good work in you will complete it until the day of Jesus Christ... (Phil. 1:6 NKJV)."

"And this I pray, that your love may abound still more and more in knowledge and all discernment... (Phil. 1:9 NKJV)."

"Let nothing be done through selfish ambition or conceit, but in lowliness of mind let each esteem others better than himself. (Phil. 2:3)."

"Not that I have already attained, or am already perfected; but I press on, that I may lay hold of that for which Christ Jesus has also laid hold on me. Brethren,

I do not count myself to have apprehended; but one thing I do, forgetting those things which are behind and reaching forward to those things which are ahead, I press forward to the goal for the prize for the upward call of God in Christ Jesus. (Phil. 3:12-14 NKJV)."

Paul was secure in who he was, and he is secure in who Christ is, and as Paul got older he was secure in his friends and in the fellowship of believers. He became the elderly statesman of the church instead of the wild-eyed radical unfit for human consumption.

Then there is John the Revelator, the last apostle to die, whose last words, according to Jerome were, *"Little children love one another."* In his last years, he was too old and ill to walk and had to be carried everywhere. Finally, after his followers had heard this statement of loving one another over and over again, he was asked, *"Master why do you always say this?"* To which he replied, *"It is the Lord's command and if this alone is done, it is enough."* [3] He knew to keep the main thing, the main thing. Upon his demise in Ephesus, he was buried in the present Basilica of Saint John, and the church and burial site can still be seen in Ephesus today. Pilgrims around the world gather there to honor this

---

[3] Tilley, A. (2020). *Communion with God and Community with Man.* Columbia, South Carolina: Kindle Direct Publishing, pp. 139-140.

follower of Christ who finished well. Moreover, it can be said that at the age of ninety-three that John, the only disciple not to be martyred, was welcomed into heaven with a *"well done good and faithful servant."* (Matthew 25:23). He gave us his loving heart and a loving salutation, and his writings are still moving us to greater works today.

So, you ask, *"How do we finish well?"* If the Biblical patriarchs can do it, why can't we? Well, you can, so let us begin to explore the aging process of ministers. However, take notice, I purposely asked not, *"How can I finish well?* but, *"How can we finish well?* You see, you cannot by yourself finish well. You will need the "us" of the church and the community of Christ to make it through this time. We must understand that anything we have done has been done in the collectiveness of God. I call it the "Us" principle of the Bible. We are not alone in this world, and we are not alone in our aging process. Many have gone before us paving the way for our success both in life and in death. In Western culture, we have a culture of individualism and then seek to stand alone and apply that thinking in the "Golden Years of Ministry." In our culture, we prize the man who all by himself climbed Mt. Everest. We give medals and accolades to the cowboy who with two six-shooters and a lot of machismo was able to defeat the entire troop of bad guys all by himself. We make a hero of David Livingstone of the mission world, who all by himself saw entire tribes in Africa converted, when in actuality David Livingstone, the great missionary from England, recorded only one convert during his entire missionary service. It was later when the others, the "Us" of the African nations, rose up and turned to Jesus that entire ethnic groups came to know Jesus. You cannot live alone, and you cannot die alone, even if the only other person there is God. This is a group endeavor and in later chapters, we will explore how we will fulfill the purpose God has prepared us for.

In Chapter Two we will focus on the initial necessary changes needed in our thinking. We must rethink and renew our lives in Christ alone. We are listening, so speak again Lord.

"Seek the Lord while He may be found, Call upon Him while He is near." Isaiah 55:6 (NKJV).

Chapter Two
What to Say, if you Talk to Yourself

If we are going to survive this "change of life" episode and finish well, then we must change the way we think. We first must acknowledge as King David did, *"I have been young, and now I am old:..."* (Psalm 37:25a) The first step is to admit that you are old, not just older. We may have to reinvent who we are and become something new, as we are not who we think we are. As illustrated in God's Word, we are constantly being molded as a potter to clay. God removes the nonmalleable shards and molds us into a vessel of honor to be used, even in our old age. In Jeremiah 18:1-4 a word picture speaks of this when Jeremiah writes, *"The word which came to Jeremiah from the Lord saying: 'Arise and go down to the potter's house and there I will cause you to hear My words.' Then I went down to the potter's house and there he was, making something at the wheel. And the vessel that he made of clay was marred in the hand of the potter; so he made it again into a new vessel, as it seemed good to the potter to make."*

Then Isaiah 64:8, reads, *"But now, O Lord, You are the Father; We are the clay, and you our potter, And all we are the work of Your hand."*

Therefore, we know that if we are going to finish well as elderly pastors, some of our old clay must be removed to be remolded into a vessel fit for His use in our older lives. How is a person supposed to change the way that one has been thinking all of one's life? We must start the rethinking process and let it take root in our hearts.

We think and learn by the written word and the spoken word. Before Moses' time, people heard about God and his word through oral tradition or the spoken word, but after Mt. Sinai and the manifestation of God through the commandments, mankind came to learn through the written word. According to Dr. Miles Jones, author of "The Writing of God," it has been proven, both linguistically and archaeologically, that the Hebrew language was the first written language and Israel was the first nation to go from a pictorial language such as Egyptian hieroglyphs to a distinct alphabet.[4] God has since spoken to us through his incarnate Word, through Him, the Word of God, and through the oral word as well. (John 1) Words have meaning, therefore we will learn in this chapter the importance of changing our thinking by changing our language and some of the words that we have been using incorrectly. This is not some magic formula, but I am going to use one example of this inaccurate word usage as an index or guide to lead us to a more realistic way of understanding ourselves at this time of life. We are going to explore how to change our thinking by changing how we speak and think through the use of new words. For example, we will illustrate this through the use of new prefixes, specifically the "dis" and "re" prefixes.

This idea of the "dis" and "re" word prefixes and their use in communication was first brought to

[4] Jones, M. (2019). *The Writing of God.*, Kerrville, Texas: Benai Emunah Publishing.

my attention when we were missionaries in the Balkans. Our Balkan director's wife, Sheryl Beard, spoke in a devotional about how language influences our thinking and our walk with God. It opened my eyes to some new concepts that changed my old thinking. Today, since we are endeavoring to learn how to grow old in ministry and change some errant thought processes and behavior, we will explore just a few ways that we can change our thinking by listening to His Word. We will learn some new ways to process our concerns about aging.

We will need to learn how to speak again to ourselves, and our souls, and use what psychologists call "self-talk." The Bible tells us, *"For as he thinks within himself, so he is."* (Proverbs 23:7 NASB). Every day we wake up with thousands of words going through our brains. We see images, we sing songs, we carry on conversations, we make plans, we develop ideas, we ask questions, and then answer them. We talk to ourselves, to God, and to others, and carry this conversation within ourselves without ever speaking a word out loud. As elderly pastors, we have a mountain of conversation and self-talk that we have accumulated. It goes around and around in our heads and after some consideration, a behavior will emerge that is either positive or negative depending on what we have told ourselves. We are full of good and bad ideas, some from God, some from ourselves, and some from

Satan himself.

Many times our minds race so much that we are unable to sleep, and we make plans from "tired" brains that feed our hearts and soul with all kinds of misconceptions.

Motivational speaker and author, Jennifer Rothchild, suggests we do more than "self-talk," we also do "soul talk." She suggests in her book, "Self Talk, Soul Talk",[5] that we talk our way into and out of troubling moments in our innermost spirit by talking and carrying on conversations within ourselves alone. We have the authority, not with just our outer tongue, but also with our inner tongue to make changes in our spiritual life and our emotional character which leads to corrective behavior. Think for a moment about the story in Mark 5 where the woman had an ailment, a long-time infirmity, to which she told herself, *"If only I may touch His (Jesus') clothes, I shall be made well."* She had spoken to no one except herself and within her being her faith arose, and Jesus healed her illness because of words spoken in self-talk to her soul in faith.

We also have the example of David in Psalm 42, where he looks within himself and asks, *"Why are*

[5] Rothchild, J. (2007). *Self-Talk, Soul-Talk*. Eugene, Oregon: Harvest House Publishers.

you downcast, O my soul? Why are you so disquieted within me?" (NKJV). David is checking in with himself and taking a moral inventory of his inner man, his soul. We can read today of his inner conversations through the Psalms that he wrote as he talked to himself and answered himself. We can read how through his self-talk he motivated himself to *"...encourage himself in the Lord"* (I Samuel 30:6 KJV).

The writer of the great hymn of the church, "It Is Well With My Soul," also found comfort and inner peace in his expression of self-talk as he wrote this hymn in a time of great personal agony. It was self-talk put to song.

Therefore, as was suggested, we are going to contrast two prefixes, "dis" and "re" and see how that correlates to changes in our golden years of ministry. We will learn in the next chapter how to compare and contrast and search our souls for the right thinking thus resulting in the right behavior.

Chapter Three
Learning to Speak English Well Again
"Dis" and "Re" Words

The prefixes "dis or des" are fascinating words as their usage is always seen in the negative in the English language. According to the dictionary,[6]

---

[6] *American Heritage Dictionary*. (1976). Boston, Massachusetts: Houghton Mifflin Company, p. 374.

it refers to invalidation, deprivation, (distrust, disuse), removal or rejection (disbar, discard), apart or asunder (distrain, digress), away or abroad (dismiss, divulge), negation or deprivation (disparage, disturb), and reversal (disapprove, disunite). The list of negative "dis" words takes up over nine pages in my dictionary with hundreds of words of discouragement and disapproval.

The prefix itself has its ancient origins in the mythology of the Greeks and Romans. In Roman religious lore, the god, Dis, (Pluto), was a god of the underworld and was connected with the dead and with wealth. Dis or Dis Pater was worshipped by the Romans and the Greeks, although the Greeks used the name, Hades, to identify him. Of course, in English, we interchange the name hell and hades as the abode of the devil and all things evil, and evil it is, whether in Greek or Latin. However, since Dis was the name of a Roman god and a Celtic god as well, it evolved into our language as a prefix for all things bad or evil. You add the prefix dis and the negation of the word is understood such as the example of the word, encourage to discourage. [7]

Why do I take the time to explain the nature of the words used? It is because I hear so many "dis" words in

---

[7] Grimal, P. (1985). *The Dictionary of Classical Mythology*. Oxford, England: Basil Blackwood, pp. 141, 171.

the language of the elderly, including the elderly pastor.

Instead of a "re" prefix, that puts a newness and a positive twist on our thinking such as reborn, redo, and reinvent, we engage in "dis" thinking that is ungodly and disheartening.

"Think about it. "Re" words have to do with returning something (a person, a relationship, a project, a universe) to its original, intended state. For example, Scripture uses a word like reconcile to describe how the relationship between God and people is made right again. But it also uses that word to describe what we are to be doing in our daily lives. We are reconciled to become reconcilers (see 2 Cor. 5:14-21). And a word like redemption describes how Christ paid for the sins of the world...In other words, the most common "re" words in Scripture are more than just repetitive words used to assure us we are headed to heaven if we trust Christ. They are also summary words that describe the role the church and the individual Christians are to play in the overall story of the world." (including elderly pastors – my emphasis). [8] (Smith and Stonestreet, 2015).

This is not some type of hocus-pocus thinking, but I am using these metaphors and prefixes to show how unknowingly you are succumbing to old-age thinking

---

[8] Smith, W., Stonestreet, J. (2015). *Restoring all Things*. Grand Rapids, Michigan: Baker Books, p. 18.

that always finds a dark cloud to every lining instead of a silver one.

We are endeavoring to "end well" instead of just end. Yet, pastor after pastor tells me, *"I am so discouraged, disheartened, disjointed, discontent, and filled with disease,"* and then they continue with a long string of "dis" words that make ministry miserable. So, with some help, let us guide ourselves through our negative thinking and turn it into a new phase of life, of ministry, that will lead us into the "golden" years as God molds us into a new creation in Christ Jesus. Let us examine the relationship between "dis" words and "re" words and their spiritual significance in the aging process of ministers. Remember "re" words are again words, asking us to once again be what we started to be.

1. Discouragement vs Renewal

Discouragement: (Disability, Disheartening)

Discouragement and despair are words equally expressed when I speak to many elderly pastors. They interchangeably tell me that they are frustrated, anxious, out of touch, and feel generally sad. It appears it is not something that they can pinpoint and actually say, *"This is making me sad,"* but they often will say, *"I don't know why I am sad, I just feel that way."* Most pastors do not have control over their feelings, because feelings can just appear, and occur because of certain behaviors that we engage in. It is a stimulus-response effect and rarely do we get to pick what comes our way. However, we can control what we do and say. We can control our behavior and our responses. Not often do we counsel with an elderly extremely discouraged pastor, who after counsel, immediately changes their feelings, and leaves the office happy, with burdens lifted, and at peace with themselves and God. It took time to take on these feelings and it will take time to take off these burdens of discouragement. We must change our thinking to start the process.

Nevertheless, most counselors will tell you: that the belief about an aberrant behavior must change before the behavior changes. Where did you begin to digress and leave the peace of God in your life? Was it a second lustful glance at the new young worship leader with a heart to yearn for younger days because you believe you must hold on to the earlier days of vitality? Was it the lack of Bible reading and study because you believe you know much of what the Bible says, and you have read it all before? And how about the loss of prayer and devotions every day? Is it because you are old and tired and excuse bad behavior with the justification that *"God knows, and He understands."* How about that bitterness that crept in over an argument with a church deacon and you believe you are right? When did sin and anger start you down the slippery slope of new behavior that drew you away from God, and you justify it by saying, *"I'm old, so just deal with it."*

You see, all of these behaviors you control. You control what time you get up. You control your exercise schedule and the diet you keep. You control the people you engage with and how. You control when you pray. You control your relationships with others. It is not the *"devil made me do it"* syndrome. You can control your behavior and since you can, you can also control the feelings that accompany that behavior. Discouragement comes when things are not going as we want them to, and since we are not in control, we lose the right perspective and the right attitude. If these thoughts are sustained, discouragement will lead to full-blown depression and you will join the long list of old bitter pastors licking their wounds. Life feels out of control and we feel we have lost our ability to control it. We lost control and we are angry. Something must be done and therefore we need to call in reinforcements of "re" words to help us recover.

Psalm 139:23-24 says, *"Search me, O God, and know my heart: try me, and know my thought: And see if there be any wicked way in me, and lead me in the way everlasting"* (KJV).

So, let us begin that search now by the renewal of our hearts and be restored and leave discouragement behind.

Renewal: (Repurpose, Restore)

Renewal begins with a behavior change, a new stimulus that will result in a new response. You as an elderly pastor must gain new insight into who you are at this moment. Nothing can be changed in the past, and the future has yet to be written. Renewal first starts with a renewal of your mind, a redo.

Romans 12:2 says, *"And do not be conformed to this world, but be transformed by the renewing of your mind, that you may prove what is that good and acceptable and perfect will of God"* (NKJV).

I saw this happen firsthand when I noticed my hometown pastor, who although just in retirement age, begin to lose what he thought was ministry. He pastored a small church in rural Louisiana and as a close friend and congregant, he confided in me one day that he was physically losing strength. I began to notice that he had a difficult time lifting anything with his right hand. He would try but he had no strength. He would struggle just to lift his Bible to the pulpit. It was not that he was out of shape, for he had been a basketball coach in the local high school and had maintained a healthy physical physique even after his retirement from teaching.

He was intellectually sharp, but his body began to fail him. Doctor after doctor sought to explain this strange physical behavior, for the loss of strength spread throughout his entire body. He worked at staying in the pulpit and preaching, but no matter what he did, the disease progressed. Finally, in desperation, he contacted a physician, a specialist in the next town, who diagnosed his illness as that of Lou Gerigs' disease. There was no cure, and ministry, his calling, and his lifetime of service were seemingly coming to an end. He believed that he would preach to his dying day, but now because of his illness, pulpit ministry was out of the question. He knew he had to radically change his behavior and his perspective on his life and ministry. We talked for hours at his home when I would visit, as he sought to come to an understanding of who he was and who God was. At times he was bitter, sorry, angry, and confused, but soon a change came over him that accompanied him to his final hour.

Pastor C. told me, *"If I cannot preach from the pulpit, I will preach from my wheelchair."* And he did just that. He opened his garage door at his home in the middle of this small town in central Louisiana, and he renewed his conviction to carry on God's work.

His wife began to make coffee and small cakes and cookies, and he began to keep ministry hours sitting in his wheelchair in the middle of the garage. He would open his garage door and sit there and invite those that passed to come in and talk awhile. He was ready for ministry again. He changed his belief thereby changing his behavior. It was not like it was before, for now, the ministry for Pastor C. was even better. More people visited him in his garage than had ever come to his small country church. He told me, *"Rodney, these are my best ministry years ever, for I get to sit at home, and not worry over the tithes, over building set-up, over parking, or anything at all, and yet people come and listen. I have had more converts and prayed for more people this last year, than in all the years before."*

The town rallied around him, loved him, listened to him, cared for him and his family, and he forever changed that town from the confines of his wheelchair. He thought and applied some "re" words instead of "dis" words, for God had done a work in his feelings and his spirit

Was he healed later? No, I am sorry to say, he was not. But Pastor C. died as he lived, as a great, humble man; a man who finished well.

His spirit was renewed, his faith redone, and his life remade into a vessel of God's doing. He delighted in "re" words, in the same words that God delights in. The master potter was at work, and instead of wallowing in his weakness, Pastor C. understood when Paul said, *"Therefore I take pleasure in infirmities, in reproaches, in needs, in persecutions, in distresses, for Christ's sake. For when I am weak, then I am strong."* (2 Corinthians 12:10).

Pastor C. has since gone to be with the Lord, but he was faithful to the end because God was faithful to the end. Did he give up? Never! Did he become discouraged? Yes, many times, but he turned his "dis" ability into a "renewal" of all things good. He was an inspiration to me and the entire town of Hornbeck, Louisiana. Well done good and faithful servant. You were faithful to the end and you finished well and we all know it. We want to be just like you and we miss you dearly.

2. Disassociate vs Reassociate (Reassemble, Replace)

Disassociate: (Dismiss, Dislocate)

I live in an over fifty-five years of age mobile home park and here everybody is old, older, or really old. I guess I am somewhat in the middle, age-wise. Since moving into the park, I have noticed how different people react to the changes in life, in their new environment. Some act out with freedom and enjoyment, some with anger and resentment, and others with isolation and loneliness. Some people are always outside tending their garden, and others are out chasing the younger residents of the opposite sex, while others have become the cat lady and have isolated themselves, never to show their face again. Some play cards every Sunday night in the clubhouse, and others, mostly men, play billiards with a little money always at stake. Some go house to house with cookies and cakes, while others ride their electric carts as if going to a Nascar meet. I thought it would be boring to live here, but it is not in the least. It just depends on your ability to socialize and keep a good attitude. It depends on whether you will subsist in the "dis" community or will you thrive in the world of "re" words.

It is the same in ministry. Ministers take the following checklist below and if they factor in five or more bullet points, they think it is over and therefore they isolate themselves to the easy chair to watch reruns of "Gunsmoke." (That was not a Christian television show, for they were always killing each other, and Miss Kitty was no angel for sure.) The checklist is taken from "The Minirth Guide for Christian Counselors" [9] and it attempts to evaluate our emotional and psychological well-being by looking at the following items:

1. Exhaustion

2. Detachment

3. Cynical

4. Irritable, inpatient

5. Feeling unappreciated

6. Change of attitude

   a. Withdrawal

---

[9] Minirth, F. (2003) The Minirth Guide for Christian Counselors. Nashville, Tennessee: Broadman Press, p.48.

    b. Increased dominance

7. Paranoia

8. Decreased concentration

9. Increased health concerns

10. Unfulfilled expectations

11. Depression

12. Suicidal thinking or not wanting to live

13. Loneliness

14. Detachment

As you can see, we could all check at least one of these boxes as we evaluate our wellness in the aging process. It is not how many boxes on the checklist that apply to you, it is rather, how are you coping with the problems that are presenting themselves and that you have checked.

For example, I have a good friend of mine who was a former pastor and missionary. He was successful in his overseas ministry and could speak the foreign language like a native. He was well known and loved by those on the mission field and by those at home in the United States as well. His family was well-adjusted and his ministry at home and abroad was a success story in missions. He was and still is a good friend, and he was a model for me as I sought to emulate his ways of ministry and his ability to form and maintain good relationships. However, as he has gotten older, he has begun to change. Instead of remaining an outgoing vibrant positive missionary, he left the field, took a secular job, and quit attending church.

He moved into his internal shell, and his family and he began to move apart as each family member struggled with the inability to maintain strong relationships. He felt unappreciated for all the hard work he had put into church ministry and felt abandoned, which at times he was, for the church administration at the state level did not maintain contact, but that is another story to be told later. He translated that lack of interaction into a *"they don't care for us"* attitude. It became a sad story of loss, withdrawal, and detachment. He is still in good health, but sad to say, his relationship with his church family has ceased to exist. He stays home and watches television preachers, and his attitude is one of cynicism and worry. He is not finishing well and since he is such a close friend, my heart mourns his loss and his lack of direction. For him, it is over.

He did not reassemble and reevaluate and replace "dis" thinking with "re" thinking. He did not replace his ideas of where he is at spiritually and emotionally and then come up with a good answer. His belief is that ministry is over. But it does not have to be that way. He is full of experiences, and good stories of success, and could be a great mission educator that we all need to hear. He has made a choice, but it feels as if he made the wrong choice because it has led him where he never wanted to go. He told me he feels so lonely, and he is.

So, what do we do? How could we help? First, we never live in a vacuum and the church should be a welcoming place for all, both young and old. And usually, it is. But what can pastors do that are in his shoes and feel his pain as well? What if your church really is a misdirected entity? How can your get redirected and made new? What if loneliness has taken control and has taken you down the pit of despair? Where do you go as an elderly pastor and find help?

Let me give you a "re" word checklist of possible solutions.

Reassemble: (Remake, Redo, Restart, Reconstruct, Relationship)

1. Refresh: Share frustrations and find support from old and new friends. Redo all those old friendships that you let go of and return to that earlier age when you dreamed with friends and planned new adventures. You may never go again on the grand adventure, but you can begin the adventure of friendship again.

2. Review: Be honest with God about your expectations and be willing to change.

3. Rethink: Correct inaccurate thinking about the past and the future.

4. Restart: Find and correct if possible, the physical ailments that plague you. Buy those bifocal glasses, get fitted for new shoes, wear the brace, stand up straight, and do whatever you have neglected to do in the past. Be proactive and find new ways of doing

old habits and reinventing new ones.

5. Relook: See the big picture and live one day at a time.

6. Revaluate: Stop the cycle of worry. Most worriers tend to live in the future that remains elusive, while obsessive pastors live for a tomorrow that never comes. And then again, depressive pastors tend to worry about the past. The Bible says, *"Take therefore no thought for the morrow: for the morrow shall take thought for the things of itself..."* (Matthew 6:34, KJV). Learn from others' mistakes. We saw what Elijah did in I Kings 19 when confronted with fear and worry. He tried to hide and isolate in a cave and drown himself in his sorrow, but God would not allow him to wallow in his pity and called him out. God fed him, spoke again to him, allowed him to rest, and then sent him out again to do God's will. He was reactivated by the presence and Spirit of God.

We must reassemble our will, our lives, our physical bodies, and our spirit and form a plan of action that is proactive and honest. Again, Minirth (2003) tells us to, *"Face the inevitable and if Not the inevitable, accept the Possible."*[10] Stop isolating and start reintegrating into the life of Christ and the life of the church. Apply all the "re" words you can and leave the "dis" behind. It is not over, simply different.

Begin to renew those relationships that brought healing and a reassociation of lives lived together in the past. Reactivate old dreams and lost memories of past successes. Redo it all again. Remake your circle of influence and make your circle bigger. I know it has gotten smaller through the years as friends and family have died off, but it does not have to stay that way.

On a personal note, I found that my circle of friends, contacts, and network of interests had narrowed to the point that my circle had almost become a dot instead of a circle. I decided to enlarge my circle by writing books. I had never authored a book before, but my friend showed me how I could write and be

---

[10]Ibid, p. 52.

published for almost nothing financially. He showed me some tools of the trade and I found that I like to write, and I have found that people are reading my books. My dot, albeit small at the beginning, became a game of connecting the dots until I found that I had come around three hundred and sixty degrees and made a circle. Now my free time is not filled with Andy and Barney in Mayberry, as I fill my free time with old sitcoms, but it is filled with reading and developing new ideas to share with others through the printed page. You might want to check out Amazon KDP (Kindle Direct Publishing) and begin to write as well and enlarge your circle and your pastoral witness to those beyond the pulpit.

3. Disappointment vs Reassess

Disappointment: (Disapproval, Disdain, Dislike)

What exactly does disappointment with God look like when you are an elderly pastor? I think it will be manifested in the idea that what you expected from God, is not what you received or experienced. You expected health in your old age and received cancer. You expected financial security, but got a stock market crash and lost all of your 401K. You expected fame and a position of influence, but all you got was a back seat on the bus of ministry. You think you did your part, but God did not do his. You expected God to be revealing himself and his master plan for your life up to the time of death, only to find that God is silent and speaks in small sound bites in old sermons and leftover notes.

You begin to compare yourself with others, but only with others that are doing better than yourself. You remember, Pastor A. who died at ninety-two while riding his bike in the gym. Now, that is the way to go! Or how about Pastor O. who is way too old, but booked with conferences for the next year? How does he do it and how did he get all the breaks? He is no better than I am, by the way, we went to Bible school together. What makes him so hot in today's market?

You measure yourself against others and whether it is life or death, you feel you are missing out on what should be happening.

But you forget the many martyrs and missionaries who passed away at a young age never to return home to America. You look at success as the world does and you always come up short. You look at success as the Christian world in America is presently doing and you come up even shorter. You compare yourself to yourself and find that God is lacking. We are asking questions of God, but He is not answering. We knew so much about God in the past and now it seems we know nothing. I do not know if I am more disappointed in God or disappointed with myself for being disappointed with God. Does God know?

Yes, as elderly pastors, we do have disappointments. In fact, whole books, such as Philip Yancey's best seller, "Disappointment with God" give you an entire treatise on reasons for disappointment and the resolve we must have to travel the long road back to sanity. However, we look at the road back and reassess the issue and think we do not have enough time left in our lives to make the long journey home. But reassessing is what we must do. We must begin again.

Reassess: (Revaluate, Renew, Remember)

First, to quote Philip Yancey, *"The Bible never belittles disappointment (remember the proportion in Job – one chapter of restoration follows forty chapters of anguish), but it does all add one keyword: temporary. What we feel now, we will not always feel. Our disappointment is itself a sign, an aching, a hunger for something better."* [11] (Yancey, 1992). And something better is coming. This world is not our home and you know it, but you must believe it. So let us begin to apply some "re" words to our disappointment.

A. Reassess: You must reassess your condition, and your situation, from God's perspective. Have you ever thought about how it feels to be God? That may sound strange but begin new, rethink from the beginning, and ask the hard questions. It may change your closed spiral of

---

[11] Yancey, P. (1992). *Disappointment with God.* Grand Rapids, Michigan: Zondervan Publishing House.

thinking into an openness of ideas. Have a friend and ministry colleague assess your spiritual well-being and with an honest face, receive his input. Have you ever entered into an honest conversation with a ministry colleague and gotten another opinion? Maybe even ask that deacon that you are in conflict with. He may have the answer you are looking for.

B. Remember: Has the last two years of arthritis negated all the seventy years of health? Have the long years of purposeful ministry fallen on deaf ears? I think the answer is negative, a no, for sure. You must remember, recall, and sometimes even regress to earlier times when life was to your expectations. Remember that first view of the Grand Canyon, and that first kiss from your wife. Do you remember the first sermon you preached that lasted all of three minutes but took you a week to prepare? Remember.

C. Renew: Renew your relationship with God that is not contingent on your ministry and what you do for Christ. It is not in the doing, it is in the being. Your health or lack thereof has not reduced God's love for you. He likes you, no, He loves you.

4. Disbelief vs Reaffirm

Disbelief: (Discredit, Discount, Disagree)

Many elderly pastors as they get older start to discard or disbelieve long-held beliefs, church dogmas, and theological concepts held in high esteem throughout all of church history. They think if they are going to keep their message contemporary they must preach and find new ideas, new theological concepts, that are hidden from the rest of the ministerial world. They will have a special revelation, a special calling, a special touch from the Lord, that their colleagues do not. As pastors get older, people find us, to be honest, out of touch, boring, and generationally lagging.

Therefore, older pastors in a reactionary mode of attack find hidden scriptures, the latest scripture numerology, or an end-times flow chart that will explain in detail the newest Middle Eastern prophecies. Instead of trying to follow the latest teaching, we will become the latest teaching, and they will follow us. We will go from post-trib., to pre-trib., to no-trib., all in an effort to keep up with the latest and the best new teaching that is emulated from the successful church pastor. We will show them that we are not losing our edge, but we are on the edge of all things new. We are successful too. But it will not take you where you want to go. It will be like the greyhound dog chasing the elusive mechanical rabbit running around the racetrack on the edge of town. It will not work. You will not end well. Leaving the truth of the gospel to follow the latest trends will keep you running from workshop to workshop, from conference to conference, as you seek to remain young in your abilities and thinking. Give it up. You are not young, and you are not the "cat's meow." Skinny jeans do not look good on a 75-year-old ex-hippy, and that baseball hat will never cover that bald head of yours even with a ponytail hanging out the back. It is okay to be yourself.

If not, you will join the ranks of pastors who use "super soakers" to anoint the congregation with holy water.

You will teach spiritual birthing as men and women get on the floor in the birthing position to birth new spiritual highs. You will have your congregation and youth run the Holy Spirit prayer tunnel as prayer warriors surround you with shouts and the laying on of hands so that you emerge out of the tunnel filled with the Spirit. You will tell the church that the Lord led you to build a drive-through prayer window where like Mcdonald's you can take their order and give them the brown bag special. You will take your prayer laser machine you perfected and shoot prayers into rocks so that the *"rocks will cry out and praise Him."* You will lead the Jericho march and give yourself a possible heart attack. You will drink the leftover communion wine and become addicted to alcohol and explain it away as just *"doing the Lord's work."* You may even start a ministry to drug addicts only to become one and then be busted on the church property for selling opiates. You will extend a loving hand to girls that are in the throes of sex trafficking only to fall in lust with the pretty new young one and fall off the wagon again. (All of these manifestations of the church I have seen personally and more). You will crash and burn, leaving a trail of ashes in your wake. Many pastors have.

So you decide not to join the latest and the greatest fads, and you take the opposite course of action and seek to discredit all things new. The song service is too loud, the stage has too much lighting and that fog machine? Are they trying to give us all asthma? Drums? They are of the devil! And who ever heard of preaching from a chair? Church on Saturday night? We are not Catholic with a Saturday midnight mass. And by the way, we do not burn holy incense in this church, but essential oils, now we sell those in our church bookstore and for a very reasonable price.

What is an older pastor to do? "Re" again!

Reaffirm: (Restart, Redefine, Replace)

Again, and again, we use the "re" words to find a solution to your individual pastoral problems. You started out right, so why not end right? You began with a dream, why not end with a vision? You started with God, then be authentic, and end with God. God is unchangeable and the truth of who God is, is anything but transient, and the facts remain the same. The packaging may be different and the faces are a little strange, but faith overcomes culture. The love from God overcomes age, and the truth of your past beliefs is only strengthened by your doubt. If you doubt your beliefs then you must believe in something greater than your doubts, and that is when you cease becoming God and allow God to be who He is.

"In the Bible, the sin of idolatry is not just a matter of bowing down to statues. Idol worship is treating the work of your own hands as if it were divine, worshipping yourself as the highest source of value and creativity. When the Second Commandment reads, "You shall not make yourself a graven image," one commentator takes that to mean not, "You shall not make an idol for yourself, but "You shall not make an idol of yourself." Do not make yourself into an object of worship by believing that you have enough power to control the world in which you live and the other

people who live in it." [12] (Kushner, 1965).

You can rest from your work, for it was God's work anyway and He does a much better job managing it. He knows all things, has done all things and has completed everything He has started. Let Him complete the good work He has started in you. (Phil.1:6 KJV).

"Sometimes in life, we have to become less to be more. We become whole people, not based on what we accumulate, but by getting rid of everything that is not us, everything false and inauthentic. Sometimes to become whole, we have to give up the dream." [13] (Kushner, 1965).

As an older pastor, you began to disbelieve in yourself, and your God. It has come to be someone else's vision and dream, and someone else's God, a God, a vision of Christ, that was not yours. So, we must reaffirm our purpose, our God-given ministry, and with the assurance that your call from God of fifty years ago will sustain you through today's call to remain faithful.

[12] Kushner, J. (1965). *When All You've Ever Wanted Isn't Enough.* New York, New York: Summit Books, p. 53.

[13] Ibid, p. 150.

You will finish well for sure.

5. Disobedient vs Responsible

Disobedient: (Dishonesty,   Disloyal, Disconnect)

Sadly, we must also address another issue and that is the disobedience and dishonesty of people in the ministry. For counselors, social workers, doctors, and nurses, ethics and continually taking ethics courses for CEU credits, is a constant reminder that those in the helping professions also need accountability. Violations of ethics standards are kept by the various states and a long list of employees have their names black-listed for ethics malpractice. You lose your license, you lose employment, and you lose self-respect. We only wish that pastors had that same infrastructure in place.

The news of late has been filled with pastors that have violated the trust of the church and have violated Christian principles, and many of those that did are elderly pastors who should have known better. The pastors were elderly, seasoned pastors who had years of successful ministry only to be caught in a web of deceit and then proceeded to lose all integrity. We all know older pastors who had illicit sexual encounters along with financial mismanagement and vice. We can name them by name, and point out all their mishaps. What went wrong? How could a man of such standing fall to such depths? We must examine that closely, for if you are reading this book, I assume that you too want to finish well and do not want to lose your very soul.

How many times have we heard an older pastor feel that he is above reproach as he reiterates over and over, *"I started this church. If anyone should know what to do, it's me."* They feel invincible and when it looks like control of the church has been lost, deacons are fired, administrations are dismissed, and all dissension is labeled heretical. Older pastors begin to quote the *"touch not the Lord's anointed"* verse and sermons become tirades of anger and hostility. It is not a pretty sight. "Dis" words such as discord, discharge, discolor, discrepancy, and disfavor, become so frequent that you assume they are reading directly from the "dis" list of words in the dictionary.

The older pastor tries to hang on to his authority and the continuation of his legacy. He will appoint his family to places of importance and significance in the ministry so as not to lose what he feels he has made and developed. We have all seen television pastors that have massed millions of dollars, and for some reason, they think it must have been my doing and my four and no more. We did it and I will not let it go. They even name the ministry and buildings after themselves and seek to pray, *"my will on earth as it will be in heaven."* It is sad, but it happens with too much frequency and the world outside of the church takes great pleasure in watching us fall. As older pastors, we must reassess our motives and make the necessary changes. If not, paranoia will set in and everybody outside of our sphere of influence will be declared an enemy. You will not finish well. You will leave a legacy of mistrust and gossip and those that knew you will leave disappointed and in disarray.

Responsible: (Reform, Redeem, Repent)

But as in all the discussions held so far, we know that "re" words will take you from the bottom of life and put you back on top of God's favor and will. It takes a reintroduction of Christ Jesus in all that you do and a reconnection to all those that you alienated including family, friends, and even that deacon that you cannot stand. You will have to take responsibility for your actions and react in ways that are Christ-like and holy. You must relabel habits that you excused and call them by what it is, sin. You must renew your life to a higher calling, to a calling beyond you and beyond your abilities. Let us face it. You are getting old and you are going to die, and all the best books, DVDs, CDs, podcasts, blogs, and leftover sermons will never keep you current and at the top of the ministry ladder of influence. Remember it is God alone.

Psalms 62: 7-12 (NKJV), *"In God is my salvation and my glory; The rock of my strength, And my refuge is in God. Trust in*

Him at all times, you people; Pour out your heart before Him; God is a refuge for us. Surely men of low degree are a vapor, Men of high degree a lie; If they are weighed on the scales, They are altogether lighter than vapor. Do not trust in oppression, Nor vainly hope in robbery; If riches increase, Do not set your heart on them. God has spoken once, Twice have I heard this: That power belongs to God. Also to You, O Lord, belongs mercy; For You render to each one according to his work."

Yes, you are getting older, and yes, you must relinquish some of your ministries. But it is okay. If you are to finish well, you must not wait until you fall out of grace, and in disgrace have to leave the pulpit. No, it must start now with you seeking to acknowledge that *"He alone is my rock and my salvation"* (Psalm 62:2) Keep reevaluating all that you do in light of the grace and peace of our Lord Jesus.

I have always heard that when you find yourself on the wrong road go back to the place where you missed the turn and begin again. Many times we want to continue down the road we are on, but just hide the mistakes and brush aside the criticism. Wrong again, we must find that "re" word that we all hate and that is the word, "responsible". We must take account of our actions, and own up to our misgivings, and our dishonesty with ourselves, with others, and with God.

Recently, I reread an old Dave Wilkerson book, "Set the Trumpet to Thy Mouth", and I must admit, it was a book that again shook me to the core and took me again to my knees. In it, he says, *"A ministry to Christ demands that we renounce hidden things of dishonesty."* [14]

And then he goes on to quote 2 Corinthians 4:1-2, *"Therefore seeing we have this ministry, as we have received mercy, we faint not; but have renounced the hidden things of dishonesty, not walking in craftiness, nor handling the word of God deceitfully; but by manifestation of the truth commending ourselves to every man's conscience in the sight of God."* (KJV)

Dishonesty is the last of the "dis" words that are listed, but one where elderly pastors should not grow confident

---

[14] Wilkerson, D. (1985). *Set the Trumpet to Thy Mouth*. New Kensington, Pennsylvania: Whitaker House Publishers, p. 107.

and think that they are above ethical considerations. We are vulnerable. We are sinful. We are mere men with tiny brains, but happily for most of the time, with big hearts. If you find yourself questioning your motivations, your desires, and your shortcomings, just as you have preached for years, come back to God. Just repent, and start again. Renew your heart, redeem your time, restore your relationships with God and man, and ask for God's regeneration.

It is okay to restart from the beginning. It is just a matter of age and the time to begin again can start even if you are ninety and beyond. Remember, if you think about it, God is very very old, ancient in fact, and He is doing all right.

Homework:

When we started this exercise in wordplay, most of you did not understand exactly where we were going, and maybe you still don't. Therefore, we are going to address other "dis" words and you fill in the "re" words that correct the incorrect thinking and aberrant behavior.

1. Disable

2. Disagreeable

3. Disapprove

4. Disavow

5. Disaster

6. Disapprove

7. Discard

8. Disclaim

9. Disciple

10. Discharge

11. Discontinue

12. Discord

13. Disfigure

We can go on and on with "dis" words that will only cause distress and disruption in your life as a pastor and as a man or woman of faith. Now that you understand, you will see "dis" words everywhere. Hundreds of them will clog up your thinking pores and reduce you to despair. But notice them, feel them, dismiss them, and be reborn again. It all started with a "re" word, "reborn", and it is really where you need to begin again. Be renewed again and again, and again.

For example, if we overlook what these "re" words

tell us about how fallen or broken the world is, we'll be tempted to live for the promises of this world, seeing health and wealth as indications of Jesus' blessing. On the other hand, if we overlook how these "re" words point us back to God's original, very good design for the world, seen instead only its evil and harmful potential, we'll make safety from this world our goal. Separation and distance become false indicators of Christian faithfulness.

But Christ's followers are to see the world differently and have a different posture toward it. Rather than safety from or capitulation to the world, the grand narrative of Scripture describes instead a world we are called to live for. This world, Scripture proclaims, belongs to God, who then entrusted it to His image bearers. [15]

We were called to be pastors, and pastors we must remain. Maybe you will not remain in the pulpit, but let ministry still reign in your heart, being subject to the original calling. You got this, you know you do.

However, there is one last consideration that must be taken into account. Certain ethical concerns must be addressed. We discussed it slightly under the "dis" word of dishonesty, but there is one word that we must address again in the "Us" of ministry

[15] Smith, W. and Stonestreet, J. (2015). *Restoring all Things.* Grand Rapids, Michigan: Baker Books, p. 20.

and that is the "dis" word: dishonor. When we fail as pastors we bring reproach not only to ourselves but to all pastors everywhere. When we lose sight of our position in the church, churches all over the world feel and suffer for our inadequacies. We are the body of Christ and when one suffers we all suffer. For example, if you are no longer doing active ministry on a full-time basis, do not take a full-time salary. If you are working as a missionary and your mission supporters think you are still on the mission field taking care of the native population and you are not, please let them know. Ethically and biblically, *"a laborer is worthy of his wage,"* or wages. (Luke 10:7) However, if you are not working, you are stealing someone else's money and using it for gain which is not ethically honest. This will bring dishonor not only to you but to the church in general as those on the outside judge us for our misadventures. How many times have pastors and missionaries quit in their hearts but remain on the payroll just for selfish reasons? You cannot go there and be blessed. Be honest with yourself, others, and God. If you do not excuse yourself from the expense account, you will one day be remembered and on some front page newspaper, you will be noted to be another dishonest pastor. The church and the mission deserve better. Honor the church, yourself, and other pastors.

The Bible says, *"And if one person suffers, all the members suffer with it, or if one person is honored, all the members rejoice with it."* I Cor. 12:26 (NKJV).

Then in John 7:18, it reads, *"He who speaks on his own does so to gain honor for himself, but he who works for the honor of the one who sent him is a man of truth; there is nothing false about him."* (NIV).

Proverbs 25:28b (NIV) says, *"...nor is it honorable to seek one's own honor."*

Chapter Four
I Am Losing Everything

We have just explored how to rethink our position, and then redo our ministry as we remake and regenerate our relationship with Christ. It is not so simple to just change the way one thinks resulting in new behavior and in new emotions to accommodate our new position in Christ. It is just not that simple.

One pastor relayed that he knows that he sounds like a whiner and a complainer, but it feels like every day he loses something else, and rethinking will not bring it back. Things that seemed certain, forever, and stable now seem to be lost in the throes of new ideas, new places, and new events that cannot be controlled.

I lost my spouse. I lost a child. I lost my parents. And now, I am losing anything that remains. At least, that is what it feels like. I am losing my strength. I am losing my health. I am losing my security. I am losing the house that I lived in for years, and now I even lost my pet. I am losing my job. I am losing my teeth. I am losing my faith at times. There is nothing that I am not losing. I have sung, *"I was lost but now I'm found, was blind but now I see"* and now I am even losing that, my eyesight. The loss is correct, but the act of finding is eluding me. Life is not fair. God is not fair. Look at the sinners and it seems and feels like they are making it fine. They have good health insurance and new cars, and sometimes even a new spouse. They are taking cruises and vacations to Europe and all I do is get a double stack of pancakes once a week at IHOP. I am old and everything is old around me. Tell me that this is not all I have to look forward to as an elderly minister: losing, and getting lost. I think I am losing my mind.

Yes, this may sound like you. I cannot deny it and neither can you. But it is not over, just different. God does understand old age, for he has been in his golden years for all eternity. Why do we always portray God in art and paintings throughout the world in chapels, churches, and museums as an old man? Because He is! He is always seen as an old man with a long white beard and fiery eyes, and with a stare that can stop the universe. Why is God never portrayed as a young man? For He is not. As we know, He is called, the "ancient of days" and who better than God to understand the plight of the elderly pastor than a God as old as the cosmos.

Therefore, let us delve into some of the losses that an elderly pastor experiences for God does understand. All of these losses that we will explore first are called primary losses as they are things or persons that are actually lost. Then we will observe the secondary losses that occur which are emotionally a result of a primary loss. These will include such losses as love, ambition, security, role, God's favor, and significance. It really does not matter if they are primary or secondary, but it is vitally necessary that one adjusts to these changes.

a. Loss of a Home:

As one matures, inevitably changes must occur. That four-bedroom, four-bath house, with an upstairs master, will not be manageable. It will be too expensive, too time-consuming, and not handicap accessible. It may have been the birthplace of your children and the home you always wanted, but you will find that it may not be the place to age well. It will be a place of great memories and those memories will remain whether you are in the house or not. Downsizing may take many avenues from a small condo in an over-55 community to an apartment in your son's backyard. Some will even buy a large recreational vehicle for the joy of being a wandering nomad with no strings attached, but beware and rent that RV for a few trips before you buy one, for it may not be what you want. No matter how large, it gets quite small and cumbersome if you live in it full-time. We want you to end well, and finish with a happy ending, and not finish in a battle of wits and sacrifices.

However, the changes come, and one of the most difficult changes is the loss of a home. Not only may you lose the home, but you may also lose the neighborhood friends that you have known throughout the years. Sometimes the loss even takes you to another state where you begin again in a totally new location. Some make the move to a retirement community, while others may make the move to a senior apartment, and much later there may be moves to a nursing facility. All of these possibilities should be discussed with family and friends, and a plan of action drawn up with financial responsibilities and your wishes put in writing. As you have heard over and over again, *"If it is not written down, it did not happen."*

So what secondary losses come with the loss of your home? Certain freedoms may be lost. Security may be lost, and for sure, control will be lost and compromised as others take over much of the decision-making for you. This is difficult for many pastors for they have always been leaders not followers and the loss of their home takes them to a lower level in their mind's eye. They are not their own. This may have been your safe place, your retreat from the eyes of the congregation, and a rest from the stresses of pastoring, and when this is lost, you will find that much of that safety net is lost as well. It must be accepted for change is inevitable and the change in housing is just the beginning. The beginning of the new you.

Gains:

Now that you are not tied to a particular house, that house that owned you, you are free to go and be where you always wanted to be. If you longed for a cabin in Colorado, well go for it, or maybe it was a beach house in New Jersey out of the rush of New York City. Now you can do just that and move and fulfill your dreams. You now can be dependent on God and God alone, and the yielding of your dependence on others gives you the freedom to be, not just do. As a pastor with a church manse or parsonage that required the elders to approve every change, you can now paint your front door red if you so desire. You can remove those old lace curtains and put up window dressings that pop as you walk in the front door. You can relax from having to be someone's idea of what pastors should be. You can now live and act and be where you want to finish your life. You can care less about "what people think." It is okay to park that convertible in the front yard instead of constantly having to drive the church van, leaving it clean and washed weekly. People expect older people to be rather odd and eccentric, so be it, and drive that Harley that you always wanted. You can even buy a boat or at least a canoe.

Less is more they say and now you can live it. A change of house and location can open up new relationships, ones based on mutual interests instead of age. The older teacher that lives down the street has now become contemporary, and the age difference now has little meaning. Once when you were a young pastor of thirty and your neighbor was aged sixty, it appeared that the chasm of age was too great to be crossed, but there comes a point in life when all older people are just the same as you are. Old becomes irrelevant. Now relationships with neighbors can be based on mutual admiration, not age, and you can become peers and equals. When you were in school a classmate in a class a few years ahead of you could not be breached, but now those people are accessible and new friendships can be gained. You did not lose a house, but you gained the world.

You are not tied to your home, your country, your state, or your boyhood home. If you want, you are free to go anywhere you want, enjoy a date with your wife, and live in the now.

b. Loss of a Vocation:

As an elderly pastor, one that is older than most of your contemporaries, job loss is very likely to occur as the congregation yearns for a younger more vibrant pastor. You may have been in the ministry for years and you feel that *"I own this church. I built this from nothing. You owe me respect and a position for life."* You feel entitled and one of the major entitlements is a job at the church in some fashion. However, we all understand that when your ministry becomes a job, instead of a calling from God, then you are in spiritual trouble. Therefore, a ministry that is not a job now, can become an opportunity for new growth in the Lord and in your life's calling. You will flounder at first with the free time you have on hand, but later you will delight in the ability to seek God in the morning, or at noon, and on wakeless nights. No time clock has to be punched and you are free to be timeless in your work. You have not lost a job, you gained a vocation, a higher call, a relationship to be lived with God at any and all times.

Gains:

By now you have discovered that your energy level is not what it used to be. You understand that some of your abilities have diminished and your memory at times is lacking, and you ask, *"How can this be better than before?"*

First, now you can focus on the meaningful, not just the dutiful. You can center your life on the inner man, not just the outward appearance. You can set aside ambition and lay the conflict of producing to another day. You can be reflective, intuitive, and excel in the issues that make a vocation worthwhile, free of the pressure of a schedule, and free to say what you always wanted to say and be. You can be all that you are in the Lord. It is great. You can gain your self-respect back by not worrying all the time about what people will think, but only about what God thinks of you.

c.   **Loss of Health:**

Paul Pruyser in the book, "Aging, Downward, Upward or Forward" helps us to understand some of the changes we make as we age. In his list of health concerns he chronicles life stages for men as follows: (women go through similar changes)

> Age 30: In most ways, he is at his peak, the tallest, strongest, and maybe the smartest he has ever been. And yet he can see the first lines on his forehead. He can't hear quite as well as he could. His skull's circumference has started swelling. His degeneration has begun.

Age 40: He is an eighth of an inch shorter than he was ten years ago, and each hair follicle has thinned two microns, but not everything is shrinking; his waist and chest are ballooning. All over he's beginning to feel the weight of time's passage; his stamina is greatly diminished.

Age 50: His eyes have begun to fail him, particularly at close range. He notices quirky changes; his speaking voice has risen from a C to an E-flat, his thumbnails are growing more slowly, and his sex life has dipped below the horizontal mark.

Age 60: By now he has shrunk three-quarters of an inch. He has trouble telling some colors apart, distinguishing between high tones, and making distinctions among the different food he tastes. His lungs take in just half what they would have thirty years ago.

Age 70: His heart is pumping less blood. His hearing is worse, and his vision is weakening. Yet if he's made it this far, say the statistics, he will live another 11 years. And if he has the right attitude, he will look back with awe at the wonders that have made him what he has become. [16]

And we know, that health issues do not stop at age seventy. It continues on a downward spiral, with heart, lung, and brain issues. Cancers and diseases arise and carry us to the brink of hopelessness, and yet we long to live just a few years more. Our bodies begin to have "body sway" and in the pulpit, it feels embarrassing, as we lose balance and coordination. We hear less and deny more, and we move to the large-print Bible for assurance. We hope we do not lose incontinence while preaching, so we take frequent bathroom breaks, and make sure we have our "pad" on correctly. It looks bad for the future as far as our physical and mental condition, and yet we are still here living in the land of the almost dead. And we ask the question again, *"What is a pastor to do?"*

Our body image changes and if our self-image is dependent on how attractive we are to others and to ourselves, we are in a struggle that will not come out positive. Self-esteem and the new norms will have to be adjusted to conform to reality. You will

---

[16] Pruyser, P. (1975). *Aging: Downward, Upward, or Forward?* in *Toward a Theology of Aging.* Liston Mills: Human Sciences Press, pp. 102-118.

have to be comfortable with the self you have become with less hair, loss of teeth, less strength, less sexual vitality, and less energy. And you ask, *"Now what is in it for me?"*

Gains:

With our new loss, what will we do? What possible gains can there be with the loss of health? Well, there are many possibilities. For one, you can begin to define yourself in terms of what one is, not in terms of what you do. You can have the freedom to seek what you want to do with the time left instead of seeking to fulfill others' expectations of what you should do. You will begin to value each day and then explore the relationships you have now, now that you are still alive, and breathing. You will find a place of thankfulness for each new day, not taking for granted your health and well-being. You will rejoice more wholly when you pray for healing for others and see God heal and confirm his presence. You will enjoy seeing your grandkids play and be thankful for their health and their presence in your life. Your attitude of placing your life and all that you are in the hands of God will bring you new peace. This will be a feeling of peace not based on what you have or what you do, but on who God is and who you are in God's family. As a pastor, you can love more without the worry of being misunderstood. They will expect you to be different, and eccentric, so fulfill their expectations. Follow the first and greatest command to love God and to love your neighbor, and do it with a clean heart and clean hands.

Remember to get your medical check-ups. Get your eyes tested. Have your teeth cleaned. Take long walks and go back to swimming. Take your weight and watch your diet. Get a good night's rest. Spend more time in prayer and study. Write a book, sing a new song, be at peace with God, and forgive. It is not over. You are still in the land of the living, so live.

d. Loss of Wealth:

By now you have tenure at church. You think you are financially secure. You saved, you invested, you bought and sold, and you are doing pretty well financially. Then medical bills set in and that last operation you had on your foot was in the six digits. Again, you ask, *"What is a pastor to do?"*

First, as discussed previously, downsizing is an option and a plus for most people since they are physically unable to maintain a large house. And that downsizing can take a variety of options as one can learn new ways of managing money that gives good investment value. Social Security will continue to provide the minimum and with a little research, you may even increase that dividend. For example, many people do not realize that veterans of the United States military can automatically increase their social security checks by filling out a simple form at the Social Security Office and providing a copy of their DD214.

As health care costs will probably continue to be your highest expense in the long term, health share companies such as Medishare and Liberty Care may provide more savings and more credible care than many of the so-called classic insurance health care providers.

We must not fool ourselves, as we get older, and we are unable to work, the available funds will be more limited. You may have to move into a group home or into a campground that provides shelter for older missionaries and pastors. Fifty-five and older mobile home parks can be another option for those with a limited cash flow. Church retirement villages are available in some states and a move may be necessary to take advantage of those privileges. Another financial perk is that a few states do not have a state income tax which can be a great incentive to make such a move. Of course, the classic money saver is moving in with your children to take advantage of their hospitality and care and using the advantages of collaborating your money into a common pool of funds.

Depending on the community, many towns and cities have food banks, social services, free medical clinics, senior centers, and community daycare, all for the use of seniors. Isolation is the great "killer" of senior life so meet with others your age and find out how they are coping. It is better together.

Gains:

You will probably ask, *"What possible gains can there be by having less money?"* For sure, less money means less income tax. Less money means less paperwork, but that does not always feel like a gain. It feels like only a necessity. However, less money does means that you will develop new relationships based on who people are, and not on what people have. For years, if we honestly access our past, many pastors pursued the big "tithers" in an unhealthy fashion. We went after the cash flow and sought to cater to those who gave more. But now, you can pursue friendships based on common interests not on the common dollar. Talk to any missionary and they will tell you that in countries with less consumerism, relationships both in and out of the church are stronger, more authentic, and with more actual community. The loss of trying to make one dollar more may be the greatest gain in your lifetime. It is freedom from "stuff" that you can't take with you anyway. Philippians 4:19 says, *"And my God shall supply all your need according to His riches in glory by Christ Jesus."* And instead of a great scripture on a plaque overlooking your desk, it will be truth written in your heart because you are living it. That is a great gain never to be lost.

Yes, there will be both gains and losses, and some will be primary and others secondary in our lives. Primary losses are the loss of mother, father, son, daughter, husband, wife, job, friend, house, health, and money. Secondary losses are the loss of love, control, self-respect, ambition, reputation, freedom, security, acceptance, role, and confidence, just to name a few. You will probably go through many of these losses as a pastor or as a missionary, but God will remain when everything else is lost and the knowledge of that truth will be a great gain. Philippians 3:18 states, *"Yet indeed I also count all things loss for the excellence of the knowledge of Christ Jesus my Lord, for whom I have suffered the loss of all things, and count them as rubbish, that I may gain Christ and be found in Him..."*

Chapter Five
Death - The Ultimate Loss in Aging

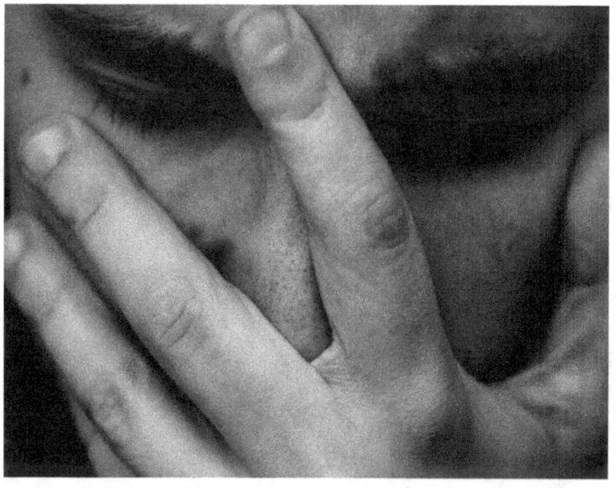

In the last few chapters, we addressed the various issues, many practical, some emotional, but all spiritual, that must be assessed for the elderly, aging pastors, and anyone in the field of ministry. In this chapter we are going to look at death and loss; the loss of a wife, the loss of a child, the loss of parents, and other losses that all ministers will have to deal with as we age. We had looked at some secondary and some primary losses but death appears to be the ultimate loss.

Just in the last month, two pastor friends of mine lost their wives. They knew it was coming and they had years to prepare as both wives had serious long-term illnesses, but both pastors told me, *"Emotionally it took me by surprise."* They are pastors who were retired, pastors who had a fantastic history of ministry, and yet they needed something more. There were no scandals, no ill-gotten gains, and no financial disasters, but emotionally they still were not prepared. I do not know if we can ever prepare, but we can be aware. What can be done? When and how? These are the questions we must face.

What does one do with grief? Where do you go? What do you say? When you are at the end of the line, the end of the rope, what should be your reaction? Tie a knot in the end and hold on as some say, I am not sure. In the book "Faith Under Fire" by the Vicar of Baghdad, the Reverend Andrew White, relates his struggles as he tried to minister to a congregation in Iraq during the Desert Storm Invasion and the sequence of events that followed. Pastor White was the Anglican priest for the Diocese in Baghdad and death there was as common as sitting down for tea with the "kettle on." On most days, death was literally out the front door of his church. He could not leave the church grounds and the church itself was bombed on numerous occasions. He quoted an evangelist he heard once who said, *"I only knew that Jesus was all I needed when He was all that I had left."* [17] And with Jesus, he made it through, scarred maybe, but not defeated. Death was commonplace but never accepted.

When you face extreme loss and the trauma that accompanies that, Jesus may be all that you do have. I have had to counsel people whose houses burned, leaving them nothing to their name, and yet with the help of faith and family, they survived and finished well. The trauma and the PTSD that accompanies such events such as the death of a spouse, the death of a child, and the loss of property can last a long time, but God is there for the long term and as stated in Matthew 28:20, in Jesus' last words, *"I am with you always even to the end of the age."*

The only problem is that in times of extreme loss, it does not feel like God is always there. I think that reflects the sentiment that I have heard from pastors and pastors' wives who have lost their spouses, and now do not know how to move forward. Overcome with grief, they felt alone, but

---

[17] Guillebaud, Simon. *Home Focus Conference*. Holy Trinity Church, Brompton, England.

not lonely, that is, until some time had passed, and the flowers were put away, the phone calls stop, and the sympathy cards stopped coming. Then, loss becomes a reality to be lived each day and into the early morning hours.

What is a pastor to do? Put on a pretty face and step back into the pulpit as if nothing happened. I think not. It does not work, but what does?

Loss has a variety of faces and death is the most universal and most obvious, but there are others that we need to explore as well as we mature into ministers in our golden years.

Let's begin to examine grief, loss, and the trauma that accompanies the emotional roller coaster.

Death:

a. Death of a Child:

The most obvious and well-documented loss in a pastor's life is the loss of a spouse or a child by death, whether accidental or natural. Contrary to what most think, the loss of a child is probably more devasting to the pastor in the long term than that of a spouse. As a parent, you always think you will die before your children, especially children who die after infancy. It is at this time of trauma that many pastors will begin to question their faith and their God, and rightly so. It is a time when the fractures that were not so evident in the pastor's marriage will begin to tear apart as each party grieves in its own way.

"How can God do this to me?" "I should have gone first." "They were so young." Or in the case of suicide, *"Why did I not see this coming?" What did I do wrong?"* Lately, some high-profile pastors have spoken openly of their conflict concerning the death of their children, especially those that committed suicide. Instead of pushing it back into obscurity, they have shown the open face of despair and anguish in the light of death and dying. Pastors in these cases are not just traumatized, but they become a victim of their guilt and grief. It is self-inflicted pain, but pain nevertheless. We know in death that the traumatized self must die so that the present-day normal self, the self that was once there, can live again. If you think you will forget about it, you never will for those memories will live on and catch you off guard at some of the most unusual times. It will be a song, a smell, or a nuance spoken

at the dinner table, that triggers an emotional response to the grief that one still carries. It may be years before a person can drag themselves out of their anger and depression, fear, and uncertainty to once again face the congregation with a settled heart and emotional stability. The pastor who survives the death of a child will carry in his body wounds that hopefully turn into scars, that although present, will not be so painful.

As Diane Langberg in her book, "Suffering and the Heart of God," explains what happens after the initial first step in trauma resolution, *"Talking, tears, and time are instruments the survivor can use to help herself to recovery. More is needed. The things we have mentioned are all focused back toward the trauma. Again, it is like a broken leg. Initially, all energy is focused on the brokenness, the pain, and what needs to be done for the leg to heal. However, if that is all the patient does, he will never walk right again. This stage (meaning the second stage) is about learning all over again how to walk through life."* [18]

This is especially true for the pastor for he

---

[18] Landberg, D. (2015). *Suffering and the Heart of God*. Greensboro, North Carolina: New Growth Press, p. 153.

carries not only the weight of his own family, but the church family as well, and the grief and trauma of loss through death many times will cause the pastor to retreat into his private world that leaves the church out. Loving relationships must be maintained to survive the loss and trauma of a loved one as dear as a child. It is at this point when the pastor is so needing outside comfort from parishioners that mean well. However, those very positive responses can lead to dependency on the congregant, instead of finding our peace from God and Him alone. I have a few pastor friends that drew close to a listening ear during these times and fell into sexual encounters that only maximized the trauma and emotional instability.

Therefore, let us look at the stages of grief and reacquaint our thinking to be aware of the loss and the consequences that accompany them. Elisabeth Kubler-Ross in her book, "On Death and Dying" (1969) listed the well-known classic list of five "stages" that one follows through the grieving process. Even though, by no means inclusive, it is a good reference with which to begin. A pastor or any parishioner will not go step by step through this list and the list is not linear, but each person will take each step according to their needs and wants.

- Denial or shock: Intellectually, bereaved people may comprehend what has happened, but their emotions may not experience pain yet; they may feel numb.

- Anger: Often this anger is released through others. The bereaved may even get angry with God. Grieving people become preoccupied with memories of what has been lost and may withdraw for a time.

- Bargaining: In the case of impending death, the grieving individual may bargain with God for more time – a time of negotiations.

- Depression: A time of sadness, and disconnection. Bereaved people beat themselves up emotionally as they blame themselves for not somehow preventing the loss. They feel disorganized and don't know how to move on with life. Depression may set in and last a while.

- Acceptance: Reorganizing their life, filling new roles, and reconnecting with those around them are healthy and important facets of the healing process. A key part of this process is the ability to learn how to feel and express the pain more truly without denial and avoidance. [19]

However, in this list of the stages of death and dying, David Kessler says the most important stage, the sixth step is left out and omitted. In his book, "Finding Meaning: The Sixth Stage of Grief," Kessler says, *"When I experienced personal grief, I wanted meaning in those darkest hours."* [20] He wanted not to accept death and dying as an end, but to understand from God's word that God puts meaning and purpose into all that we do.

"It is God who works in you to will and to act in order to fulfill his good purpose." (Phil. 2:13 NIV). Even in death, God is at work in us.

---

[19] Clinton, T. and Hawkins, R. (2009). *Biblical Counseling.* Grand Rapids, Michigan: Baker House, p. 131.

[20] Kessler, D. (2019). *Finding Meaning: The Sixth Stage of Grief.* New York, New York: Scribner.

Knowing what you may feel will help you to feel and understand that it is okay to act out emotionally. It is a healthy response to such a loss and grievous situation that has occurred in your life and in the life of your church. It may be time to find a Christian support group that will listen and will share memories and emotions that they too have experienced. It is good for you and it is good for them as well.

Many pastors have found solace in the story of David and Bathsheba after the death of their first son. David did not find consolation from others, his wife, or himself, but he did find consolation in the understanding that in the end, *"I shall go to him..."* (2 Samuel 12:23). David was confident so much in this fact that he did not fast for his lost son as many thought that he should, but David knew that his son was in the hands of God. He found peace in God and God alone.

"Precious in the sight of the Lord Is the death of his saints." (Psalms 116:15 NJKV).

b. Death of a Spouse:

Usually, the death of a spouse is coupled with a lot of "What if" questions. What if I had only been there? What if I had known earlier about the tumor? What if I had listened to the doctor? What if they did not work so hard? And the list continues. Along with the "What if" questions, guilt, and the blame game start, with first the blaming of yourself, then the blaming of the hospital, the doctor, and the medicine, and finally ending with the blaming of God. He did this. We try not to express or say it, but it resides in the back of our minds like some brainless glue that will not go away. We do not know where it comes from, but it is there nonetheless.

We have anxiety and sleepless nights, and we watch mindless television, filling up our days by staring at the walls. We think we hear our spouse's voice and do automatic responses as if he or she were still in the house. We make that second cup of coffee and then realize there is no second cup. We play mind games and tell everyone, *"Now that I do not have to take care of -------, I can go and do want I want to do"*. The only problem is that you do not want to do anything. You always wanted to go and see the Grand Canyon and so you go and all you see is a big hole in the ground. It is what we call "professional loneliness." It is a very trying time physically, emotionally, and spiritually for the single elderly pastor.

So, what is a pastor to do?

1. First, grieving is a normal response and all that you are experiencing is not abnormal. You are not going insane and you do not have a mental illness. You must begin by accepting that this is what it is and it is final for this side of heaven. There is hope for the future, but like most, you do not know what that hope looks like and that is okay. Heaven is still real and your spouse has made her home in heaven. You did make promises before they died, but you made promises to a living person, not to one who has passed on, and many of those promises cannot be kept. That is okay too.

2. Get in touch with your feelings and feel. Hurt, cry, yell, grieve, and even laugh if you can. You do not have to become bitter, but better, better at showing the real you. You will be better at expressing authenticity in the pulpit and at home. Find Jesus in a new way. Allow the Holy Spirit to comfort you and give you peace.

3. Don't act as if the deceased is still living. They would want you to go on with your

life. This does not mean forgetting the wonderful things that were done together, but do not leave the clothes in the closet and the shoes under the bed. Remove the toothbrush from the sink and let the comb with the hair attached be cleaned and put in a safe place. You are not disrespecting your spouse, you are only facing reality as it will be until you pass away as well.

4. Find value in your daily activities and stay active. Get back in the pulpit, for you still have something to say. You now know how a lot of the elderly in your congregation feel and you can empathize with them.

5. Continue to cultivate new friendships and find new hobbies outside of the home.

6. Renew your purpose, rededicate your life, and redo areas in your life that you have neglected. (You should remember this from the "dis" and "re" chapter).

7. Physically, regain your strength and start a new workout routine. Take long walks. Get tired.

8. Remember the good times and the

qualities you so admired in your spouse. How is your life better for having had your spouse in your life? Live again with memories to support your future ambitions.

June Hunt in her book, "How to Handle Your Emotions" finds an acronym to use by relating the letters of the word "C-O-M-F-O-R-T" to steps in the healing process.

"C" Come to God for all your comfort.

> *"Praise be to God and Father of our Lord Jesus Christ, the Father of compassion and the God of all comfort."* (2 Cor. 1:3).

"O" Open your heart to the reality of pain.

> *"In our hearts, we felt the sentence of death. But this happened that we might not rely on ourselves but on God, who raises the dead."* (2 Cor. 1:9).

"M" Maintain a clear conscience by confessing past sins and offenses.

> *"He who conceals his sins does not prosper, but whoever confesses and renounces them finds mercy."* (Proverbs 28:13).

"F" Find the positive in the grief process.

> *"See what this godly sorrow has produced in you: what earnestness, what eagerness to clear yourselves, what indignation, what alarm, what longing, what concern, what readiness to see justice done. At every point, you have proved yourselves to be innocent in this manner."* (2 Cor. 7:11).

"O" Obtain comfort from those whom God will send to you.

> *"God, who comforts the downcast, comforted us by the coming of Titus."* (2 Cor. 7:6).

"R" Reinforce your faith by giving comfort to others.

> *"God comforts us in our troubles so that we can comfort those in any trouble with the comfort we ourselves have received from God."* (2 Cor. 1:4).

"T" Trust in the strength of Christ in you for the power to rebuild your life.

> *"I can do everything through him who gives me strength."* (Phil. 4:13). [21]

---

[21] Hunt, J. (2008). *How to Handle Your Emotions.* Eugene, Oregon: Harvest House Publishers, pp. 245-246.

It is said that time heals all things, but in reality, it does not. It only makes their memories of them more difficult to remember. You grow older and the pain of loss grows older too.

c.   Death of a Parent:

- Shock: As an elderly pastor, you thought that by now you would be the last on the list to pass away in the family. But for some reason, you are both a parent to your children and a parent to your mother or father. You are filling a role that you are unprepared to fill and have been doing so for several years. It feels strange for now you are old, they are old, and you are wondering who takes care of whom. You think I should be retired and yet three generations and sometimes four are now living, and I am playing grandpa, parent, great grandparent, and still trying to pastor a church. What is a pastor to do? But now, your parent or parents are passing and you are caught by surprise. Even if you saw it coming, it is still a shock to you. It is a loss and a deeply emotional one at that.

  As in the death of a spouse or a child, the first step in the death of a parent will be initial disbelief. As you have always had your parents with you since birth, not having them present will be a real shock to you emotionally and spiritually. You will perceive that you are in a sense of unreality as if it is a dream or nightmare and you will awaken soon and it will all be over. You ask yourself, "How can a person be present and in the moment, and then in the next minute they are gone." [22]

The shock will subside in a week or so, and reality will set in. Your mind may play some tricks on you as hearing your parent's voice or seeing a person who reminds you of him or her. But that too will dull over time and life will go back to the normalcy that you are more familiar with.

- Despair and Depression: After the initial shock, a pang of sadness or depression will catch you by surprise, for you thought, that since they were much older than you, you were ready, okay with it, prepared, and it was just a new stage in life. But it is not.

Depression is a coping mechanism that allows you to distance yourself from the

---

[22] Myers, E. (1997). *When Parents Die*. New York, New York: Penguin Books, pp. 17-18.

event and then reorganize your thinking and your emotions to handle the rest of the life change that you just experienced. It does not feel like a sufficiently correct response, but it is a normal outcome of an event that shocked you and your family.

- Guilt and Anger: If you did not get to correct past wrongs and find forgiveness over time, you will find yourself amid guilt and regret over how you could have done better. You could have telephoned more. You could have told her that you love her. You forgot to send her that birthday card. You feel you fell short of what you as a pastor, a man of God, and a minister who knows about these things, should have done. I know others may not respond in a godly way, but I should have. I am guilty and I know it, and then anger sets in. Anger at yourself, anger at the situation, anger at the loss, and then anger towards God.

You ask, "How can I be angry at someone who is dying or already dead?" I understand that it was not their fault but I want to blame someone. Often we will blame the medical team that helped, the church that seemed to help, and the other family members who appeared to not help at all. Remember it is over and if you want to blame someone, blame the devil. Satan is wanting to keep you from being the example of Christ that as a pastor you should be. Anger may be real but in the long term, it is not appropriate. Let it go and get back to loving God and others as Christ has loved you.

- Relief: As an emotion that seems out of place at the time of death, relief is an act of your will that appears likewise, out of place. I should not be relieved that my parent has died, but since this book is about the life of an elderly pastor, your parents will be even older. It is okay that they pass away after a long life of gracious living. We will only go through death once and you have only one shot to get the emotions right for the moment, so take the test and pass. It is an open-book test, and the Bible has all the answers. Read, remember and take a rest, and let relief be a sign of God's goodness. As the song goes,

"All my life you have been faithful.

All my life you have been so so good.

With every breath that I am able.

I will sing of the goodness of God." [23]

The Bible tells us that even in death he will not forsake us, *"For I am persuaded that neither death nor life, nor angels nor principalities nor powers, nor things present nor things to come, nor height nor depth, nor any other created thing, shall be able to separate us from the love of God which is in Christ Jesus."* (Romans 8:38-39 NKJV). Live it – believe it.

Practical Steps in the Healing Process:

Homework:

- Take care of your basic needs. Eat well, clean the house, water the yard, feed the dog, take your medicines, get a haircut, and wash the car, and the dishes. Last and most important: make the bed. Making the bed sounds so trite, but if you make the bed, you probably will not return to bed and waste your time in self-pity and remorse.

---

[23] Danielson, D. (2022). A song performed on July 23, 2022, at Impact Church, Kerrville, Texas.

- Do not isolate yourself from others and remove yourself from social interaction. Get back into ministry and do it well and end well. Visit your children and grandchildren, and do not forget old friends.

- Remember the scriptures and renew your devotional time. Find times of quietness, not silence. There is a difference. One is intentional and the other is just there.

- Find the others who were also affected by the death of the child or spouse and seek solace together. They need you and you need them. Community is more than a concept.

- Do something that you enjoy, "just for me" and make it part of your routine.

- Find a safe place, a resting place, a place of solitude, that allows you to begin again. It may be a small chapel, a place by the sea, or an overlook in the mountains. Make it your special place.

- Find God in a new way. Find God in a new place. Find God in old familiar areas that once satisfied your longing for Him. He is still there.

- Write a tribute to the one that you lost. Let it be full of funny anecdotes and trite memories of daily life. Make a log from day one and continue to the present, highlighting the vacations, the children's antics, the jokes gone south, and the remembrances of days long ago. Put in some pictures, and scrapbook letters, and add a few songs and tiny tidbits of past conversations over a cup of tea. Then share the tribute with others so they too can add their memories and not forsake their applause as well. It is your memories, so do not forsake them. [24]

d. Your Death:

Since you are reading this book, we assume you are not dead. Dying maybe, but dead you are not. Therefore, we will not dwell as long on this subject as we did on other losses. Arthur Becker makes the point that *"When one has made one's peace with death so that it is no longer feared or denied, one finds a new freedom and zest for living."* [25] We will look at our own death

---

[24] Rainey, D. (2005). *The Best Gift You Can Give to Your Parents.* Little Rock, Arkansas: Family Life Publishing, pp. 95-97.

[25] Becker, A. (1986). *Ministry with Older Persons.* Minneapolis,

through the lens of the living. When the chains of death were broken by Christ and we understand that we too have been released from the sting of death, we now live in a new awareness of the resurrection and the Easter message.

Dr. Albert Outler in "Aging as a Spiritual Journey" made this observation about his coming death:

"Death is, I take it, the ultimate deprivation. I worry a great deal, for I do not see how to insure a graceful exit. This is the remaining problem....what is a graceful exit? The degree of indignity that comes with old age and helplessness, the dependence upon and bother to others seems to me to be graceless. This I dread more than anything that I can identify...Getting out of life is more difficult than getting in – certainly for the person himself or herself. But as for what it will take to ensure this, I do not know." [26]

In all the other losses through death, nothing is as personal and soul-searching as one's own death. When death approaches, the

Minnesota: Augsburg Press, p. 69.

[26] Outler, A. autobiographical statement quoted in Bianchi, *Aging as a Spiritual Journey*, p. 245.

person you have becomes the person you could have been and that is a humbling encounter.[27] We are never prepared and we, like all those that have gone before, want to leave this life in a dignified passage that is both relevant for the dying and those left behind. In our Christian tradition, we believe it is God alone who controls where and when we die. So we ask the hard question, "Is it wrong to pray for a person's death including our own?" We quote the phrase taken from Job that reads, *"The Lord giveth and the Lord taketh away."* So if that is the case and we believe it, why do we insist on the medical establishment to keep us alive? This is such a complex issue for the elderly pastor so no one answer is enough. It will force us to look to Jesus and his Word for the answers that delude us.

Pastor David Jeremiah of the Shadow Mountain Community Church is facing this same problem as he ages and he writes: *"Although loss is a four-letter word, it is not always a bad term. Jesus said, "He who finds his life will lose it, and he who loses his life for My sake will find it." (Matthew 10:39). We should be happy to lose some*

---

[27] Kelly, M. *Life is Messy*, North Palm Beach Florida, Blue Sparrow Publishing, p. 150.

things in life, for those losses become our gain. As Paul tallies up the ledger of his former life in Philippians 3, he admits that what he once considered his assets have moved to the liability column and now add up to a gigantic zero...For the apostle, the "cargo" of his past life had to be thrown overboard so he might be saved and gain his spiritual life in Christ. Do not be afraid to let go of things that keep you from God. And when the Lord takes your life, do not waste your time in regret. When God allows you to escape Sodom, do not look back. When God asks you to suffer for Him, count it all joy." [28]

Death is all about exits and entrances. You leave one place and you arrive at another. You leave the inside of your house and go to the outside world. You make passages all through life. You exited from your youth and entered adulthood. You leave the single world and enter the married world. You exit school and enter the job market and the working world.

And with Christianity, you leave the old man and take up a new man. The exit of

---

[28] Jeremiah, D. (2013). *The Jeremiah Study Bible, New King James Version*, Nashville, Tennessee: Worthy Publishing, p. 1660.

death is really the entrance into a new life. We leave a good place to go to a better place. We leave old relations to take on new relations, and we leave best friends to find the best friend we have ever had, Jesus. We leave our family to join the family of God. [29]

Revelation 21:3-5b brings it all to a conclusion, *And I heard a loud voice from heaven saying, "Behold, the tabernacle of God is with men, and He will dwell with them, and they shall be His people. God himself will be with them and be their God. And God will wipe every tear from their eyes; there shall be no more death, nor sorrow, nor crying, There shall be no more pain, for the former things have passed away." Then He who sat on the throne said, "Behold I make all things new."* (NJKV)

---

[29] Birk, R. (1996). *What's a Nice God Like You, Doing in a Place Like This?*, San Marcos, Texas: Golden Goat Publishers, p. 111.

Chapter Six
It is Time to Prepare

Old age has come and you know it by now. But again, looking for a positive answer, and hope to hang on to, you ask, "What is a pastor or missionary to do?" I am certainly convinced that I am old and getting older by the minute, but how can I get prepared? What can I do today that will make sure I finish well? To be honest, it is time to prepare now. Get ready, be open, listen, and then hear what God has planned for you again. If you were in the Army it would be time to "re-up." (There are these re words again.)

First, learn the new terms that accompany the aging population whether it is for the man on the street or the newly retired pastor or missionary. For example, know the difference between palliative care and hospice care. Learn the intricacies between Medicare Plan A and Plan B and how to maneuver between Medicare and your Healthcare provider. Know about life Insurance and long-term care insurance. Research the resources available to elderly people in your community. Is there a community care facility that is open to everyone or is it just by membership only? Do I need to apply for "meals on wheels" or do I get help from the food bank? Who is my power of attorney? Have I made a will and is it updated? Have I picked out a funeral home and an order of service? Have I spoken to my family and had "the talk," the talk about all things dark and dreary, the talk no one wants, and the talk reserved only for the last night of Christmas vacation? There is still so much to understand and so many questions that need to be answered.

You need to understand the decisions you must make medically that will arise at your time of aging such as:

- Use of emergency treatments to keep you alive.

- Will CPR be administered if you are in a medical emergency?

- Do you want to be on a ventilator?

- Is artificial nutrition (tube feeding) an option as well as artificial hydration (IV or intravenous fluids)?

- The use of comfort care and pain management and when?

- Do you have an advance directive telling what the doctors can and cannot do?

- Do you have a living will?

- Have you named a durable power of attorney for health care and has it been notarized?

- Are you an organ or tissue donor?

- Do you have a healthcare proxy and an alternate as well?

- Have you made an official advance directive and has it been legally verified and witnessed?

I know this all sounds so negative, but there are some positive things that you can do as well.

- You can write your spiritual memoirs concerning your legacy for your children and grandchildren. You can start now by collecting pictures, retelling family events, and bringing the past to life.

- You can engage the mission community as well as the church community with prayer, giving offerings, welcoming the lost, and mobilizing future generations of pastors and missionaries.

- You can be an advocate for all things Christian both in and out of the church.

- You can still dream. As a songwriter with the group, "Regenerations," once wrote, *"The dream never dies, just the dreamer."* Few people are more miserable than a once-fired-up Christ follower who stops singing and quits dreaming.[30] Fall in love with your calling again.

- Make sure that your ministry is a life-long call that in some form or another can continue to the day you die.

- Form a new community of believers that believe in God and believe in others. Don't do it alone, and then engage any pastors, both old and young, that will walk this path of ministry together with you.

[30] London, H. and Wiseman, N. (1994). *The Heart of a Great Pastor,* Ventura, California: Regal Books, p. 84.

Chapter Seven
Well Done Advice

(All of the following articles on aging are original with editing for only spelling and clarification.)

By: Otto Wegner, Church Planter and Inner-City Pastor, New Jersey.

I've been thinking, a lot. It's been more than 56 years since the Michigan District presbytery decided I passed the "test," a two-year novitiate when ministry skills are observed and fitness for ordination is determined. Recently graduated students of theology are ready for anything, overflowing with certainty about everything, and are full of world-changing dreams. Retired pastors are full of stories, many embellished by failing memory and frequent repetitions, and less certain about most things they once knew for sure. I've been thinking because when I look at myself, when I mentally and spiritually crawl around into secret places of my soul, the Holy Spirit helps me be honest. Was I ever as good as I thought myself to be, or as I led others to see me? Were my motives always pure? What happened to all the certainties of youth? Who printed "ORDINARY" on my resume? I am thinking! How do I contribute to my friend's ambitious project?

While crawling around the inner parts of my soul, I noticed a big truth tucked away in a crevice that had been etched by the time I had spent alone with my Creator. He had inspired His Apostle to write words that were meant to be a challenge to all, "For you were once darkness, but now you are light in the Lord. Live as children of light (for the fruit of the light consists in all goodness, righteousness, and truth) and find out what pleases the Lord." (Ephesians 5:8-10) As a student, those few words helped me understand my life mission, and Pat and I lived with that insight, to please the Lord. Retirement does not void the clearly stated imperative. In our experience, the change of pace, different responsibilities, or new address only caused us to find out what pleased him at our new address. And we found it!

The second discovery secreted away in the depths of our souls, Pat's and mine, was how to best continue our primary activity described by the same Apostle, Paul, in his same letter. The calling is to every Christian and preceded our vocational calling. Our Creator whispered truth into our souls, *"Be very careful, then, how you live--not as unwise but as wise, making the most of every opportunity, because the days are evil. Therefore, do not be foolish, but understand what the Lord's will is. Do not get drunk on wine, which leads to debauchery. Instead, be filled with the Spirit. Speak to one another with psalms, hymns, and spiritual songs. Sing and make music in your heart to the Lord, always giving thanks to God the Father for everything, in the name of our Lord Jesus Christ."* (Ephesians 5:15-20) We must always continue to be worshipers! Our responsibility to bless others with presence and praise did not expire. We did our best to do what was asked of us. Every opportunity is worthy to be fulfilled cheerfully, eagerly, with loyalty toward Him and the family of God. Yes, every opportunity deserves genuine gratefulness and joyful generosity. Do you remember the old ditty, "Smilers never lose, and grumblers never win, so let the sunshine in!"

That's wisdom for those who teeter toward grumpiness!

And maybe I ought to enlarge on another Pauline axiom in Ephesians when I try writing for my friend, for those who want to finish a life of ministry well. The apostolic advice is, "He who has been stealing must steal no longer, but must work, doing something useful with his own hands, that he may have something to share with those in need.." (Ephesians 4:28) Giving is Christ's followers' most natural activity. "Stingy" isn't even in the Christian lexicon. Paul says, "If you were a thief, quit stealing, work, and give." In a world of me-first, get-what-you-can-as-often-as-you-can, the Christian is a beaming light into the darkness because Christians LIVE TO GIVE! Retirement doesn't change that. Aging isn't an excuse! I wearied our congregations with, "Dogs bark, fish swim, lions roar, and Christians give!" Shortly before Pat passed away we were praying and I heard myself asking, "Lord, we'd love to give more to missions, please increase our capacity." And He answered our prayer! The small spirited stingy semi-saint holding on to God's blessing will wilt and whine into crabbiness!

I believe the One whom we are called to please, the One who called us to service and worship, the One who has led us through many seasons of life doesn't change our calling, just the way we fulfill it.

One last word, His calling in this time of our life is as satisfying and joyous as any we've known. I awake early with joyous anticipation. By the way, the world has always had a full roster of grumpy old people jockeying for convenient parking spots. Too many crabs searching for another entitlement clog the arteries intended to deliver joy and peace. Nasally challenged complainers who disrupt healthy conversations with whines and whimpers probably listen to too many of television's angry and rude talking heads. CHEER UP FRIENDS, THE ONE WHO CALLED US TO FOLLOW HIM HAS NEVER CHANGED! Let us review His calling regularly.

By: Rick Malm, Pastor, Educator, Missionary, and Director – "Commission to Every Nation," Kerrville, Texas.

"If you see me going down or I begin getting in the way, please just tell me so I can step aside." That request came from a friend of mine who had seen pastors and other leaders stay long past the time they should have passed the baton to the next generation. I could relate to his concern as I too have seen leaders who handed off the baton with grace and I've seen those who refused to let it go.

It broke my heart as I watched a mentor of mine who refused to let go of the baton. I wanted to allow him to continue to input into the ministry I was leading but every time I did it did not go well. I finally just had to determine I would honor him personally but had to limit his involvement in the ministry. Though he had been an outstanding team captain he had never learned to be a support team player. So, he collected a few faithful supporters who would follow his drum beat and he marched off into greater and greater obscurity.

Now that I've had to hand off some ministry opportunities and I'm approaching the time when I need to pass the baton in other areas, I can understand my mentor's reluctance to let go. In a relay race, the excitement is all at the finish line. I want to keep running till I cross that line. I have had all this experience and my relationship with the Lord has never been deeper and richer. What I have to pass on is of greater value than at any time in my life. Now is the time to begin, not the time to end. Especially when I see that those with their hands out to take the baton are so immature, so clueless, so … so much like I was when I was first handed the baton.

As I have watched those who transition well and those who did not transition so well, I have noticed a key difference. It had to do with where they found their identity and their source of personal affirmation. We all need to feel significant. There is nothing inherently evil with that. But those who find their identity in ministry or leadership, find it hard to let go. *"If I'm not holding the baton how will people know I'm significant, that I'm not just a spectator in the stands? How will they know I make a difference; I matter?"*

But those who find their identity in relationships – primarily with the Lord but also with family, friends, and others – rather than title or position, do not need ministry accolades to feel their life matters. Another mentor who beautifully modeled moving from center stage to support staff cautioned me, "Leadership is temporary. You could lose your ability to speak or lead tomorrow so don't ever look to that as who you are, or you will always be on shaky ground. Your identity must always be who you are in Christ Jesus."

As a young man, that always seemed like ethereal, what-the-heck-does-that-mean counsel but as I've aged and watched the results of those who tried to find identity in any other source I've begun to understand the wisdom and rock-solid practicality of that advice. Realizing you probably won't value it any more than I did in my younger years, I would pass the same wisdom on to any young ministers who are interested in being marathoners in ministry and not just sprinters that burn out after a few years of overexertion in an attempt to create a legacy for themselves.

By: Jaime Maldonado, Hospice Chaplain, Missionary, and Minister, Dallas, Texas.

As a hospice chaplain, I was asked to write about how to end well in ministry. It appears there are fewer and fewer people who make it to the END and more and more believers who are falling by the wayside, giving up on their faith. This short passage is about those who make it to the END. I have known both, those who end well and those who have not.

It appears that at the end of life, as we know it, as it is drawing to a close, there are two words that Jesus spoke in Matthew 24:10-12 about ending, the first word is <u>many</u> as in, *"...many (not just some or a few) shall fall away from the faith."* The second word is <u>most</u>, as when Jesus spoke and said, *"Because of the increase of wickedness, the love of most will grow cold. But the one who stands firm to the end will be saved."* (Matthew 24:12-13). That reminds me of Matthew 10:22, *"They that endure to the end shall be saved."*

The sign of a great falling away is the end-time sign as noted in the book of Revelation. The Apostle John is told to write to the seven churches. His instructions to each of them all end with the thought, "TO OVERCOME." Those who overcome or complete their race shall receive the prize at the end of the race.

1. To the Church in Ephesus: "Whoever has ears, let him hear what the Spirit says to the churches. To the one who is victorious, I will give the right to eat from the tree of life, which is the paradise of God." (Rev.2:7)

2. To the Church in Smyrna: "Whoever has ears, let them hear what the Spirit says to the churches. The one who is victorious will not be hurt at all by the second death." (Rev.2:11)

3. To the Church in Pergamum: "To the one who overcomes, I will give some of the hidden manna." (Rev.2:17)

4. To the Church in Thyatira: "To the one who is victorious and does my will to the end, I will give authority over the nations." (Rev.2:26)

5. To the Church in Sardis: "The one who is victorious will, like them, be dressed in white. I will never erase that person from the book of life but will acknowledge that name before my father and his angels." (Rev.3:5)

6. To the Church in Philadelphia: "The one who is victorious I will make a pillar in the temple of my God. Never again will they leave it. I will write on them the name of my

God and the name of the city of my God, the new Jerusalem, which is coming down out of heaven from my God; and I will also write on them my new name." (Rev.3:12)

7. To the Church in Laodicea: "To the one who is victorious, I will give the right to sit with me on my throne, just as I was victorious and sat down with my Father on his throne. Whoever has ears, let them hear what the Spirit says to the churches." (Rev. 3:21,22)

I grew up in a Hispanic home of thirteen, eleven kids, and my parents. I was the third oldest, I had an older sister Rachel and an older brother Raul. I don't know why but I was branded the "bad one" in the family. I was the one fighting, running the streets, and always looking for trouble. My father, Santana, was an alcoholic, he drank until he died in his mid-eighties. One example of how bad his alcoholism was, as he was getting sicker and unable to care for himself, he was placed in a nursing home, and one day he ran off. The facility was beginning to panic because they couldn't find him anywhere. They called my mother, and she told them to check any nearby bars and sure enough, they found him in the first bar they checked. They brought him back to the nursing home, but at the next opportunity, he snuck out again and went back to the bar. This time when they brought him back they put him in a more secure unit where he was unable to get out. He died shortly after being put in the secure unit; he had lost all will to live if he couldn't get to the bar.

I share that story because I was following in his footsteps. I started drinking early in my teenage years, and my father would buy my friends and me all the alcohol we wanted. The only rule he had was that we were not allowed to leave the house after we started drinking. Can anyone guess how long that lasted? I can't remember a single time when we actually followed that rule. Once we had started drinking we wanted to go out and find others to drink with. I usually returned after getting in a fight, bruised, and beaten up. Drinkers don't make good fighters, except for the fact that the more I drank the less pain I would feel. I would always come home after a night of drinking. We had a room with a mattress on the floor for all of the kids to share, and I would come in and fall onto that mattress, and pass out until I woke up sometimes hours later, other times a few days later.

It was at this time that I decided to join the military. God used the military as part of his plan for my salvation. I left home at 17 and joined the army. My mother had to sign a waiver so I could join before I was 18. When God found me I was a more intense version of my younger self. I was full of anger, rage, brokenness, and heartache. I was 22, stationed in Oberammergau, Germany as part of an MP unit. We spent our days guarding different buildings and locations, and our nights and weekends drinking and doing drugs. There was nothing about me that I was proud of. I was empty. I had been married the year before and we had one son by this point. They stayed stateside while I went ahead and prepared for them to come. Later they would join me but that did not deter my partying.

Along with the military, God also used a young man named Rodney Tilley to lead me to Christ. I was at the end of my rope by then, I would join a group of MPs and almost every weekend we would go to one of our homes and get high or drunk. I remember very clearly how I would spend those nights. I would find a dark corner in the house and bring a bottle, and I can remember thinking to myself there has to be more to life than this, more to life than alcohol and drugs. It was the same every single weekend until God brought Rodney along. We worked together and he witnessed to me about Christ, and for the first time in my life, someone told me about Jesus and his love for me. I could share dozens of stories of bad behavior, selfishness, and sin. I sometimes cannot believe that I've made it this long still in love with Jesus and want to please him as much now as I did when I first met

Him.

Here is some advice from my Father in Christ. When I was young and sadness came my way or heartache and pain overcame me, I would dull it with alcohol, but now as a child of Christ, I began to change. I learned that I don't have to respond with drinking and doing drugs. Now I go to Jesus, and I break before him, I throw myself on his grace and mercy, and he responds by loving me and telling me it's going to be ok. I know that he loves me and accepts me even with my flaws, although I am still working on them. I believe if we stay in love with Jesus, we will make it to the end. Remember one of the verses I shared, a sign of the end, is the love of many will grow cold. It's not just about our love for others or ourselves growing cold, but it is that the love of many will grow cold towards God.

As a hospice chaplain, I have been able to share with many dying patients, and those that end well are those who end well with Jesus. You must not grow cold, but if you want to end well you must end well with a heart in love with Christ our Lord, whether it is in the ministry or not.

By: Mike Cave, Pastor, Director of "Commission Ministers Network," Kerrville, Texas.

- Why do some of our ministry contemporaries and co-laborers "finish well" the race set before them, while others, unfortunately, come limping across the finish line disillusioned, resentful, and even bitter with their life of ministry?

- Mindful of my daily need for God's enabling grace, after 35 years of pastoral ministry and now directing an international network of ministers and ministries, I would like to offer several observations and recommendations for encouragement to avoid burnout and fatigue.

- Be committed to TEAM MINISTRY.

  - Don't become a "one-man show"; after all, this is about Him.

  - It has been wisely written, "Two are better than one because they have a good reward for their labor…"

- When it's time to "hang up your cleats" do it graciously.

  - You may no longer be the quarterback or signal caller, but you can cheer from the sidelines, coach or be a support to the "first team" out on the playing field.

- Tossing a grenade over your shoulder as you exit seldom ever edifies or engenders unity and well-being.

- Remember, happiness is a choice.

  - Often the crisis, and turning point situations faced in public ministry are God's way of giving us a "life message".

  - These "breaking for making" experiences can become defining moments in our calling and life journey.

  - God is using all our struggles to conform us to the likeness of Christ, so don't waste your sorrows.

- Become a "father in the faith" to those He entrusts to you.

  - I was fortunate to have had numerous spiritual fathers/mentors/coaches whom God used at strategic moments during my pastoral years.

  - God used them to show me the way and avoid many pitfalls along the journey.

  - Now we can help shape and encourage younger emerging leaders as they travel the pastoral pathway.

- Remain humble and pliable, receiving God's great grace to embrace this transitional time.

- Jesus made Himself of NO REPUTATION, taking upon Him the form of a servant.

- We would do well to imitate Christ.

Pray often for God to help keep your heart soft and tender. Walk in forgiveness, reminding yourself regularly of the promise from Philippians 1:6 that the One Who began a good work in you will perform and complete it. By His Indwelling Spirit may we FINISH WELL!

My ministry has been as a local church pastor, serving five different churches over the years. One of those was for a total of 20 years. Each of these assignments was in either rural churches or small towns. Until my wife and I became empty-nesters, I was bi-vocational. Now in our elder years, we enjoy God's continuing faithfulness.

By: Rev. Kenneth Stanfill, Pastor of 50+ years, Sectional Presbyter for Louisiana Ministers Network, Assistant Sectional Presbyter, Winnfield, Louisiana.

I have learned that to finish well, one must decide what retired minister one wants to be when that time comes. I always wanted to be the old man everyone wanted to hear preach. Well, I got half of it – the old man part! I miss both the preaching and the preparation for preaching. Opportunities do come … often in the form of a funeral … but occasionally to fill the pulpit for a church. That means I have learned to sit under another's ministry by guarding against being nit-picky about anything a pastor does or doesn't do, recognizing that the pastor has the message for that day, and attending corporate worship with an attitude to listen and respond.

Attitude is important here. I'm learning to accept that some pastoral friends mean well to say that they would like me to preach for them, but they do not follow up to schedule it. I understand that some have ministerial staff that needs the opportunity to preach. And if someone is paid staff, why add to the church's financial overhead by having a "fill-in" while someone is already there? I've chosen not to be negative about it because I want to be a retired minister that is joyful.

Having flexible expectations are also important. I didn't plan for it, but my role has become more of a mentor to younger pastors who serve in a similar context to my past. I get phone calls and visits with questions they have, their need for a sounding board, or occasional advice. I was blessed with having worked with the public since my first job at age 12. This gave me the opportunity to learn people skills that can't be learned any other way. This was extremely helpful for me in full-time ministry and now I can teach and coach others in this area.

In deciding what kind of retired minister one wants to be, I suggest that before retirement starts have a hobby. Retirement will give you the time to do things you didn't have the time to do before. A man in one of the churches I pastored refinished furniture. I wanted to learn the craft so I would help him. My "helper's pay" was the experience, knowledge, and skills that I gained. In retirement, this hobby has saved us money and provided a few extra dollars along the way.

After fully retiring, some ministers pick up a job that helps financially. This was the case for me for a short time. It also gave me a way simply to be out doing something. This relates to deciding what retired minister one wants to be because for some the job becomes almost another career. Maybe your retirement years are to be a time being used by the Holy Spirit in new ways unrelated to your previous ministry.

From my perspective, finishing well begins with living and serving responsibly from the start of one's ministry. On the home front, my wife and I always enjoyed each other's company and were close over the years. When the time came that I would be home with her much more than in the previous years of marriage, it was only a brief adjustment for us because of the years of enjoying a healthy marriage.

Financially, serving rural and smaller churches meant that we always had to budget and manage our money well. Entering retirement with few funds other than Social Security to depend upon meant continuing the same management lifestyle. (Only one church we pastored was financially strong enough to contribute to a retirement fund for us for a season.) Four of the five churches we pastored provided a parsonage for our family. Thankfully, we had enough foresight to keep the small house we had built earlier in our marriage for a place of our own when we retired. It was challenging to do so, but God has always been faithful over our years!

I think finishing well involves not being caught off-guard about one's relationship with God. Once the pressure and demands of pastoral ministry and preaching are no longer felt, one may no longer as heavily feel the need for prayer. It isn't that I do not pray now, but I no longer have a set time and place. I pray with as much intensity, but perhaps not the same duration. This has been an adjustment because it makes me feel at times that I'm not as close to God as before retirement. The reality is that I intercede more for others while my personal prayers are expressing my desire to be available to the Lord to use me as He chooses.

Finishing well is also about seizing the other opportunities retirement provides. There is time for family, grandchildren, and great-grandchildren. My wife and I enjoy each other's company. We appreciate God's continual faithfulness to us. Health issues are part of this season, but God has enabled us to both remain physically active … but slower!

Chapter Eight
Conclusion

We have tried to discover the secret to ending well in life and in the ministry. In conclusion, you may feel that now, *"age is just a number,"* and it is for many who refuse to acknowledge the new you as life transitions to old age. You also may be feeling the same as expressed by the one author who wrote, *"I am too young to be this old,"* as one book title reads.[31] You may just push it all aside and agree to *"Don't Sweat the Small Stuff ...and it is all small stuff.* [32] There are literally thousands of cliches and book titles that one hears every day about old age, such as, *"60s are the new 40s,"* as well as others, *"You are only as old as you feel,"* and *"I'm as old as dirt."* But all the cute book titles do not get you to the point of the actualization of the fact that you are getting older day by day, and you must make adjustments. We struggle to adapt to the aging process but for the pastor and missionary, it appears to be even more difficult. We refuse to believe we are having, "senior moments." We are God's elect, therefore, we are special, privileged, and have favor. And I guess we are, just like all believers, because of God's grace and love. But also like all believers, aging is going to happen and it already has.

There are hundreds of books about aging, dying, and disease, but in this book I want us to be honest with ourselves as pastors, missionaries, and ministers. I do not want us to take the way of the world and adapt it to the high calling of pastoral ministry. There is hope for the hopeless pastor and a way that is authentic, true, and lived out in an act of obedience.

---

[31] Smith, P. (1997*). I'm Too Young to be This Old*, Grand Rapids, Michigan: Bethany House Publishers.

[32] Carlson, R. (1997). *Don't Sweat the Small Stuff...and It's all small stuff,* New York, New York: Hyperion Publishers.

Paul speaks of it in Philippians 3:12-14, *"I'm not saying that I have this all together, But I am on my way reaching out for Christ, who so wondrously reached out for me. Friends, don't get me wrong: By no means do I count myself as an expert in all of this, but I've got my eye on the goal, where God is beckoning us onward – to Jesus. I'm off and running, and I'm not turning back."* [33]

It goes back to another "re" word. We must rediscover Jesus. Rediscover ourselves. Rediscover our calling. Rediscover our passion. Rediscover life as an older person. We must rediscover the joy in serving Jesus. Contrary to an earlier chapter where all "dis" words were negative and the "re" words were positive, discover and rediscover are both positive words. You started out well on your discovery of Christ and you can end well on your rediscovery of Christ again.

If you will believe this, and I am sure you do, pray with me the Prayer of Thomas Merton:

Dear God,

I am not sure where I am going. I do not see the road ahead; I cannot be certain where it will end. I do not really know myself: sometimes I fool myself, pretending to follow your will, yet

---

[33] Peterson, E. (2018), *The Message Bible*, Colorado Springs, Colorado, Nav Press

knowing I am not. But I believe this: that the desire to please you does, in fact, please you. I hope I have this desire in everything I do. I know that if I do this, you will lead me by the right road, though I may not know it at the time.

Therefore, I will trust you always and I will never be afraid because you will never leave me to face my troubles alone.

Thank you, dear God, for all you have given me; for all you have taken from me, and for all you have left me.

Amen! [34]

FINISH WELL. IT IS WORTH IT. YOU CAN DO IT. IT HAS ALREADY BEEN DONE.

---

[34]Prayer of Thomas Merton, American Cancer Society.

Addendum

Growing Old Gracefully (A Prayer from the Pastor's Wife)

Dear God:

Here I am. As I write this, my feelings are fluctuating. Who would have thought a few years ago that ___ and I would be off the farm and living in a retirement community? Never dreamed of it, even.

I miss our home of nearly fifty years. But we're here – not only in our new place but in a new place in life, older and less independent than we once were. I know this suits our abilities, and I want to be content with the way it is, not looking back at the way it was.

I am so grateful, God, for your tender mercies – new every morning. Already so many good things have occurred. We've met friendly neighbors. There are almost unlimited opportunities for helping others through volunteer work. It's also safe here, and there is plenty of time for fun and socializing. I can plant a small garden. There's help just around the corner in case of an emergency, and the surroundings are quiet and beautiful. It feels good sometimes to sit, to be still, to know that you are in charge of our lives.

Yes, I can live a full life here with other Christians who share my love for you.

Lord, you have supplied all our needs in abundance even into old age. (Phil. 4:19). [35]

---

[35] O'Connor, K. (2003). *Help Lord! I'm Having a Senior Moment,* Ventura, California: Regal Publishing, p. 225.

Additional Books by Allan Rodney Tilley

A History and Guide to Biblical Sites in Cyprus

Communion with God and Community with Man

The 38 Days of Christmas Devotional

Biblical Hospitality: The Chain that Links Fellowship to Faith

Finding Christ in Muslim Lands

I Know Nothing and Other Lessons I Learned by being on the Mission Field

A History and Guide to Biblical Sites in Cyprus – Large Print Edition

Terceira The Lilac Island – A History and Guide to Terceira Island of the Azores Archipelago

***All books are available on Amazon.com or your Kindle device.*